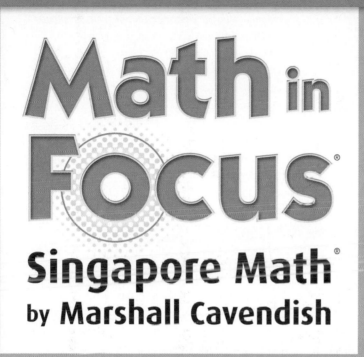

Math in FOCUS®
Singapore Math®
by Marshall Cavendish

Consultant and Author
Dr. Fong Ho Kheong

Authors
Chelvi Ramakrishnan and Bernice Lau Pui Wah

U.S. Consultants
Dr. Richard Bisk
Andy Clark
Patsy F. Kanter

Marshall Cavendish
Education

U.S. Distributor

Houghton
Mifflin
Harcourt

Published by Marshall Cavendish Education
An imprint of Marshall Cavendish Education Private Limited
Times Centre, 1 New Industrial Road, Singapore 536196
Customer Service Hotline: (65) 6213 9444
U.S. Office Tel: (1-914) 332 8888 Fax: (1-914) 332 8882
E-mail: tmesales@mceducation.com
Website: www.mceducation.com

Distributed by
Houghton Mifflin Harcourt
222 Berkeley Street
Boston, MA 02116
Tel: 617-351-5000
Website: www.hmheducation.com/mathinfocus

First published 2015

Math in Focus® Student Book 1A
ISBN 978-0-544-19355-0

Printed in the United States of America

1 2 3 4 5 6 7 8   1401   20 19 18 17 16 15
4500463696   A B C D E

Contents

Look for **Practice and Problem Solving**

Student Book A and Student Book B	Workbook A and Workbook B
• **Let's Practice** in every lesson	• **Independent Practice** for every lesson
• Put on Your Thinking Cap! in every chapter	• Put on Your Thinking Cap! in every chapter

CHAPTER
2 Number Bonds

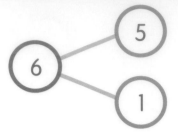

Look for **Assessment Opportunities**

Student Book A and Student Book B	Workbook A and Workbook B
• **Quick Check** at the beginning of every chapter to assess chapter readiness • **Guided Learning** after every example or two to assess readiness to continue	• **Chapter Review/Test** in every chapter to review or test chapter material • **Cumulative Reviews** eight times during the year • **Mid-Year** and **End-of-Year Reviews** to assess test readiness

CHAPTER

3 Addition Facts to 10

CHAPTER 4 Subtraction Facts to 10

Ordinal Numbers and Position

CHAPTER 7 Numbers to 20

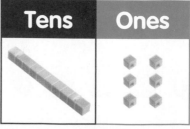

CHAPTER 8 Addition and Subtraction Facts to 20

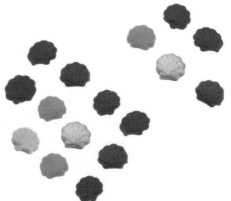

CHAPTER 9 Length

Welcome to

Math in Focus®

This exciting math program comes to you all the way from the country of Singapore. We are sure you will like all the different ways to learn math.

What makes *Math in Focus*® different?

- **Two books** You don't write in the ▭ in this textbook. This book has a matching **Workbook.** When you see  ON YOUR OWN you will write in the **Workbook.**

- **Longer lessons** Some lessons may last more than a day, so you can really understand the math.

- **Math will make sense** Learn to use number bonds to understand better how numbers work.

In this book, look for

Learn	Guided Learning	Let's Practice	ON YOUR OWN
This means you learn something new.	Your teacher helps you try some problems.	Practice. Make sure you really understand.	Now try some problems in your own **Workbook.**

Also look forward to *Games, Hands-On Activities, Put on Your Thinking Cap!,* and more. Enjoy some real math challenges!

What's in the Workbook?

Math in Focus® will give you time to learn important math ideas and do math problems. The **Workbook** will give you different types of practice.

- *Practice* problems will help you remember the new math idea you are learning. Watch for this ON YOUR OWN. in your book. That will tell you which pages to use for practice.

- *Put on Your Thinking Cap!*

    Challenging Practice problems invite you to think in new ways to solve harder problems.

    Problem Solving gives you opportunities to solve questions in different ways.

- *Math Journal* activities ask you to think about thinking, and then write about that!

Students in Singapore have been using this kind of math program for many years. Now you can too — are you ready?

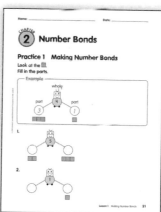

1 Numbers to 10

One, two, three, four,
Hear the mighty ocean roar!
Five, six, seven, eight,
Time to play, so don't be late!
What's next? Nine and ten.
Let's start all over again!

BIG IDEA

Count and compare numbers to 10.

1

Recall Prior Knowledge

Counting

The toys are matched to show the same number.

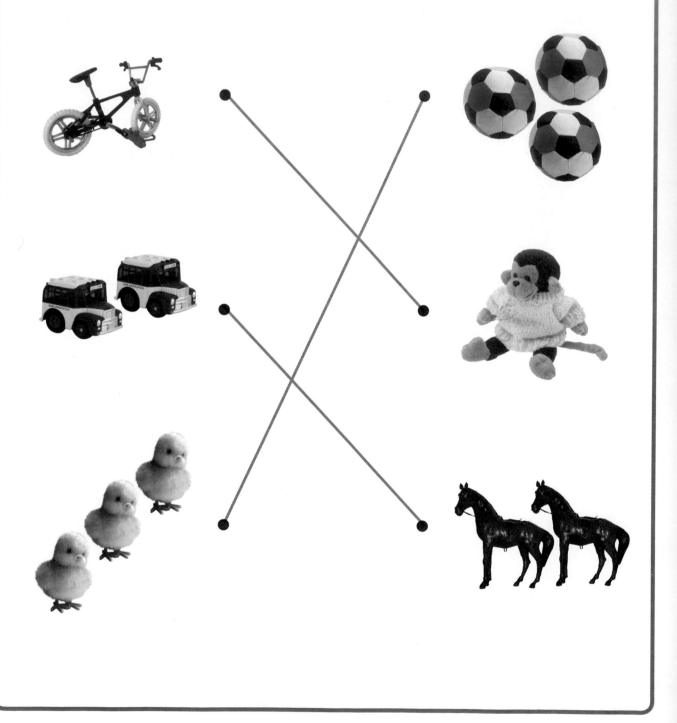

Match the  to the  to show the same number.

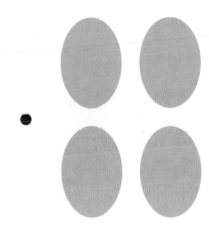

LESSON 1 Counting to 10

Lesson Objectives

- Count from 0 to 10 objects.
- Read and write 0–10 in numbers and words.

Vocabulary

zero	one	two
three	four	five
six	seven	eight
nine	ten	

Learn Point with your finger and count.

0
zero

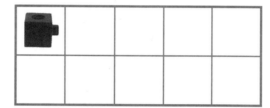

1
one

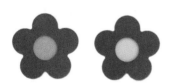

2
two

3
three

4
four

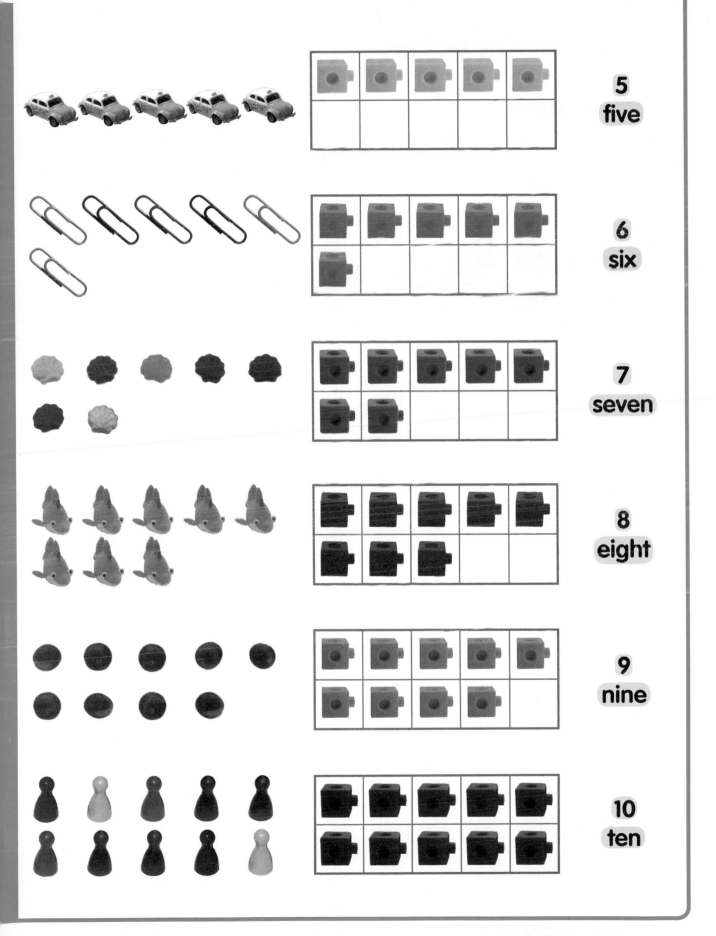

5
five

6
six

7
seven

8
eight

9
nine

10
ten

Hands-On Activity

Use .

Place a on each picture of a .

Then count.

1

2

3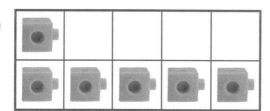

Now put the correct number of  on a ▭.

4 8

5 10

Guided Learning

Count.
Write the number.

Example

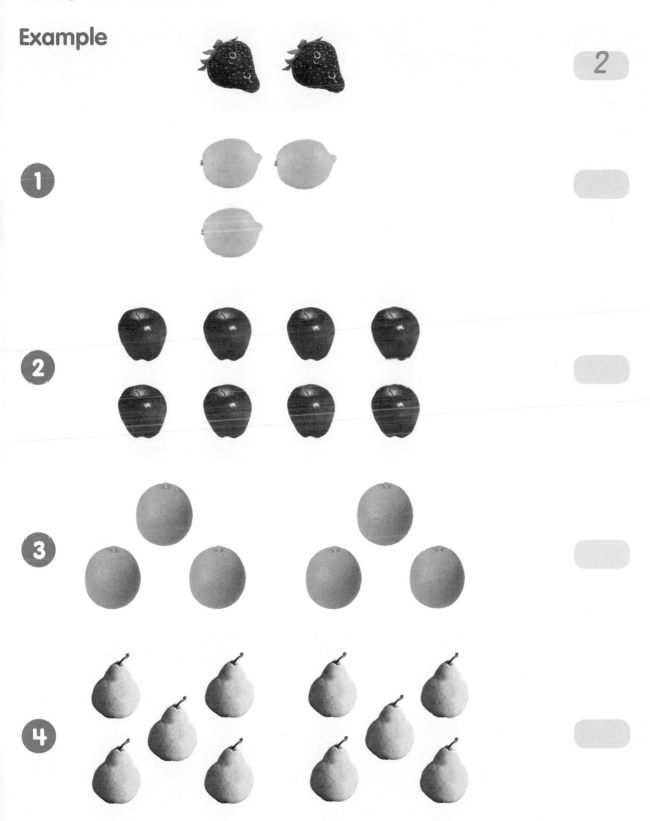

2

1 ____

2 ____

3 ____

4 ____

Point to the bugs and count.
Write in numbers and in words.

Example

3 three

5

6

7

How many are there?
Count. Write the number.

 Let's Explore!

Work in groups of 3 or 4.

STEP
1 Pick a number from 2 to 10.

STEP
2 Use  to show your number in a ☐☐☐☐☐.

Example

5

STEP
3 Then find other ways to show this number.

Example

5 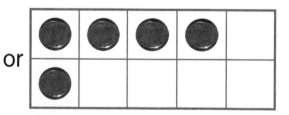 or

STEP
4 Carry out **1**, **2**, and **3** again.

Use a different number.

 **WORKING TOGETHER** **Game**

Land on 10!

Players: 3

How to play: Use only 1, 2, or 3 fingers to count.

 STEP 1 Player 1 starts counting from 1.

 STEP 2 Player 2 counts on.

1, 2

3, 4, 5

STEP 3 Player 3 counts on.

6, 7, 8, 9
Oops! 6, 7, 8

End

The player who lands on 10 wins!

9, 10.
I win!

Let's Practice

What is the number? Count. Write the number.

1

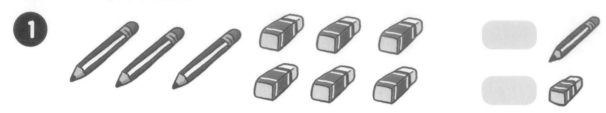

2

3

ON YOUR OWN

Go to Workbook A:
Practice 1, pages 1–6

LESSON 2 Comparing Numbers

Lesson Objectives

- Compare two sets of objects by using one-to-one correspondence.
- Identify the set that has more, fewer, or the same number of objects.
- Identify the number that is greater than or less than another number.

Vocabulary

same

more

fewer

greater than

less than

Learn Match and compare.

     There are 4 children.

      There are 4 apples.

The number of children and the number of apples are the **same**.

     There are 4 children.

     There are 3 apples.

There are **more** children than apples.
There are **fewer** apples than children.

Hands-On Activity

Use a copy of these socks and shoes.

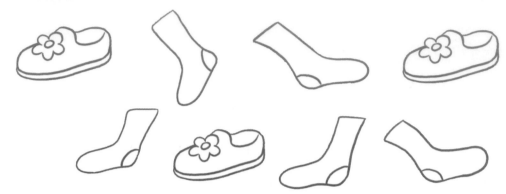

STEP
1 Cut the 👟 and 🧦 out.

STEP
2 Use two ▭▭▭▭▭▭.

Paste all the 👟 in one ▭▭▭▭▭▭.

Paste all the 🧦 in the other ▭▭▭▭▭▭▭.

STEP
3 Match and compare the number of 👟 and 🧦.

Write **more** or **fewer**.

There are ⬜ 🧦 than 👟.

There are ⬜ 👟 than 🧦.

STEP
4 Carry out STEP **1**, STEP **2**, and STEP **3** again.

Use a different number of 👟 and 🧦.

Guided Learning

Match and compare.
Write more or fewer.

1

There are [ ] than .

There are [ ] than .

2

More or fewer?

There are [ ] than .

There are [ ] than .

Hands-On Activity

This is a number train.

Use to make number trains.

1 Make a number train with more than 3 ⬛.

How many ⬛ are in your train? ▢

2 Make a number train with fewer than 3 ⬛.

How many ⬛ are in your train? ▢

 Use 🟦 to count and compare.

5 — 5 is **greater than** 3.

3 — 3 is **less than** 5.

Guided Learning

Find the missing numbers.

3

▢ is greater than ▢.

▢ is less than ▢.

4

⬭ is greater than ⬭ .

⬭ is less than ⬭ .

 Hands-On Activity

Use 🧱 to make number trains.
Then answer each question.

1 Make a number train using 4 ▢ .

2 Make a number train using 9 ▢ .

3 Compare 4 and 9.
Which number is greater? ⬭
Which number is less? ⬭

Answer each question.
Use number trains to help you.

4 Which number is greater, ⬤7 or ⬤4 ? ⬭

5 Which number is less, ⬤6 or ⬤9 ? ⬭

Let's Practice

Solve.

1 Point to the two groups that show the same number.

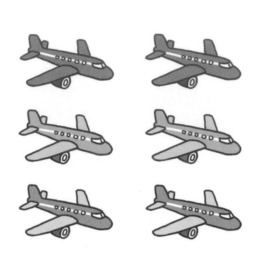

2 Which tank has more fish, A or B? ▢

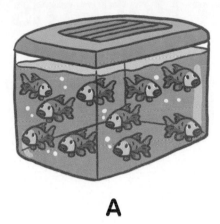

A

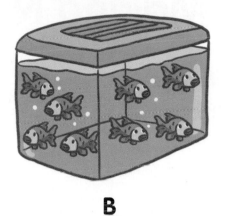

B

3 Which box has fewer chicks, A or B? ▢

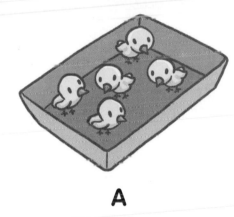

A

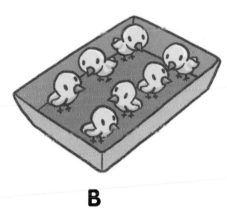

B

Which number is greater?

4 (2) or (4) ▢

5 (7) or (3) ▢

Which number is less?

6 (9) or (8) ▢

7 (5) or (6) ▢

ON YOUR OWN

Go to Workbook A:
Practice 2, pages 7–12

3 Making Number Patterns

Lesson Objective

• Make number patterns.

Vocabulary

pattern

more than

less than

Learn — Make a pattern.

Joe makes the **pattern** below using .

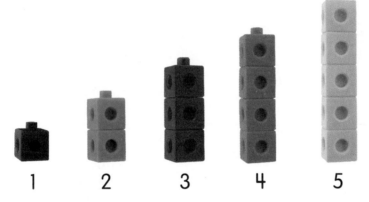

1 2 3 4 5 ?

How many come next in the pattern?

1, 2, 3, 4, 5, **6**

6 come next in the pattern.

Guided Learning

Solve.

1 Megan makes a pattern with beads.

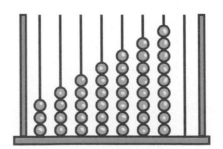

How many beads come next in the pattern?

2 John makes a pattern.

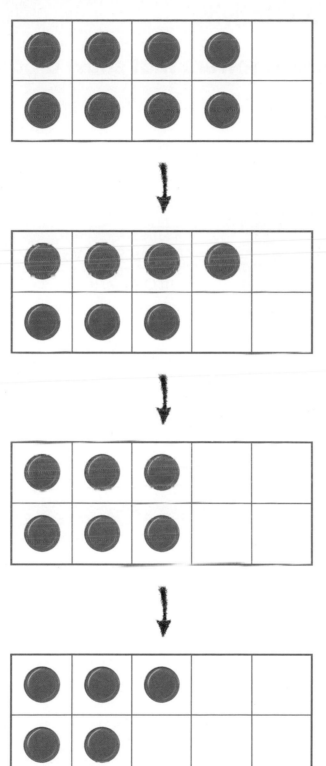

How many ⬤ are there in the next ⬚⬚⬚⬚⬚ ?

Hands-On Activity

Use  to make towers that show a pattern.

Example

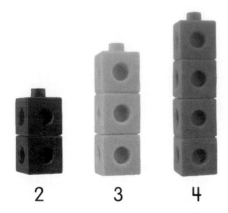

2   3   4

This shows a pattern from 2 to 4.

1 Show the pattern from 4 to 7.

2 Show the pattern from 9 to 6.

Guided Learning

Solve.

3 Count on.
Find the next number in the pattern.

1, 2, 3, 4, _____

3, 4, 5!

4 Find the missing numbers in the number patterns.

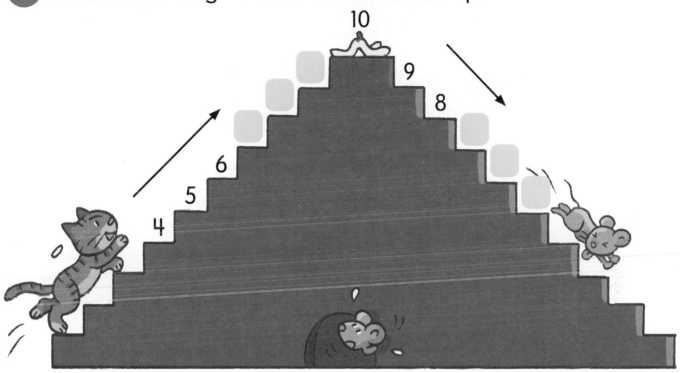

10
9
8
6
5
4

Use 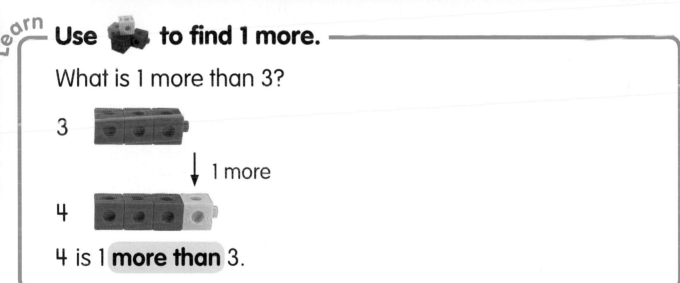 to find 1 more.

What is 1 more than 3?

3

↓ 1 more

4

4 is 1 **more than** 3.

Guided Learning

Solve.

5 What is 1 more than 8?

_____ is 1 more than 8.

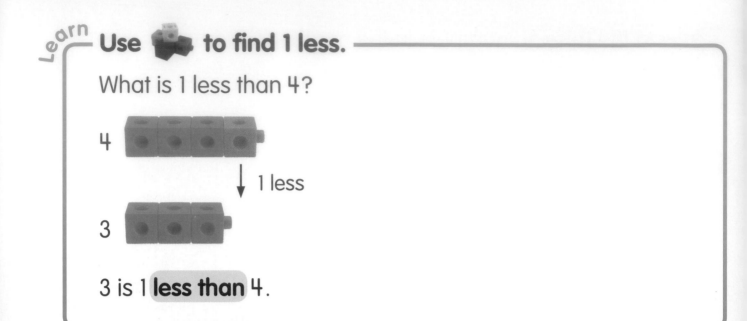

Use 🧊 **to find 1 less.**

What is 1 less than 4?

4

↓ 1 less

3

3 is 1 **less than** 4.

Guided Learning

Solve.

6 What is 1 less than 6?

[____] is 1 less than 6.

Count and answer.

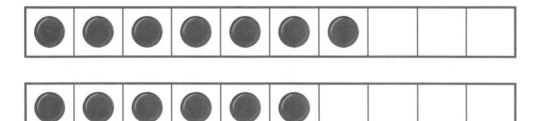

7 [____] is 1 less than [____].

8 [____] is 1 more than [____].

Let's Practice

Solve.

1 1 more

1 more than 5 is ⬚ .

2 1 less

1 less than 5 is ⬚ .

3 1 more than 7 is ⬚ .

4 1 less than 8 is ⬚ .

Find the missing numbers in each pattern.

5 1, 2, 3, ⬚ , ⬚

6 2, 3, 4, ⬚ , ⬚ , 7, 8

7 ⬚ , 7, 8, 9, ⬚

8 10, 9, ⬚ , ⬚ , ⬚ , 5, 4

9 5, 4, 3, ⬚ , ⬚ , ⬚

ON YOUR OWN

Go to Workbook A:
Practice 3, pages 13–16

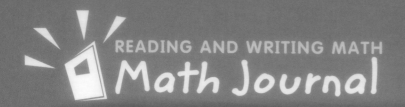

READING AND WRITING MATH
Math Journal

Which sentences are true?

1 A bicycle has 2 wheels.

2 A cat has 4 legs.

3 5 is more than 7.

4 8 is 1 less than 9.

CRITICAL THINKING SKILLS
Put On Your Thinking Cap!

PROBLEM SOLVING

Here are some counters.

Group the numbers this way.

Numbers Less Than 5	Numbers from 5 to 7	Numbers Greater Than 7

What can you say about the counters in each group?

ON YOUR OWN

Go to Workbook A:
Put on Your Thinking Cap!
pages 17–18

Chapter Wrap Up

You have learned...

BIG IDEA

Count and compare numbers to 10.

Numbers to 10

Count · **Read and Write** · **Show** · **Compare** · **Make Patterns**

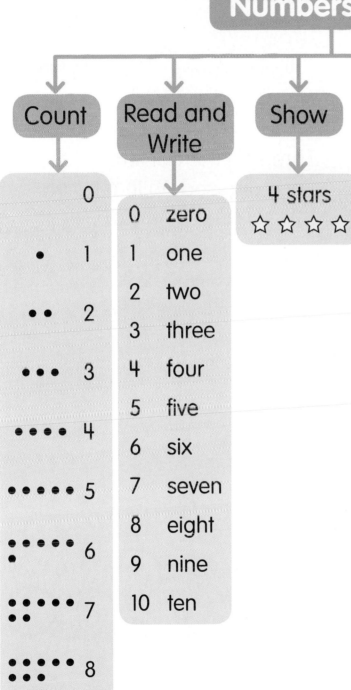

Count

0

• 1

•• 2

••• 3

•••• 4

••••• 5

••••• • 6

••••• • •• 7

•••• • ••• 8

••••• •••• 9

••••• ••••• 10

Read and Write

0 zero
1 one
2 two
3 three
4 four
5 five
6 six
7 seven
8 eight
9 nine
10 ten

Show

4 stars

☆ ☆ ☆ ☆

Compare

◆◆◆◆◆◆◆◆

▲▲▲▲▲▲▲

There are more ◆ than ▲.

There are fewer ▲ than ◆.

8 is greater than 7.

7 is less than 8.

1 more than 7 is 8.

1 less than 8 is 7.

Make Patterns

5, 6, 7, 8, 9

4, 3, 2, 1, 0

ON YOUR OWN

Go to Workbook A:
Chapter Review/Test,
pages 19–20

Kittens, kittens, cute little kittens,
How I love them so!
Seven on the inside,
Three on the outside,
Each dressed up in a bow!

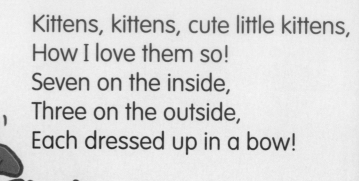

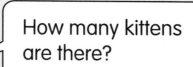

How many kittens
are there?

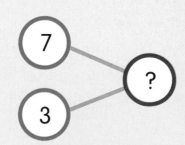

Lesson 1 Making Number
Bonds

BIG IDEA

Number bonds can
be used to show parts
and whole.

Recall Prior Knowledge

Counting

There are 5 .

1 2 3 4 5

This is a number train of 4 .

What is the number?
Count.

1

2

LESSON
1 Making Number Bonds

Lesson Objectives

- Use connecting cubes or a math balance to find number bonds.

- Find different number bonds for numbers to 10.

Vocabulary
part
whole
number bond

Learn

You can make number bonds with .

You can use a number train to make number bonds.

Sam put  into two parts.

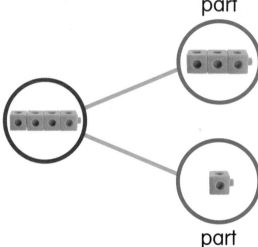

part

part

How many are in each **part**?

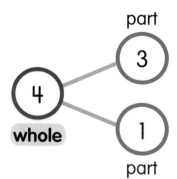

3 and 1 make 4.
This picture shows a **number bond**.

Hands-On Activity

Use  .

What other numbers make 4?

1 [_____] and [_____] make 4.

4 — 0

[_____] and [_____] make 4.

4

What numbers make 5?

2

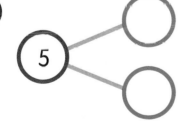

5

5

5

You can make number bonds with a math balance.

4 and 3 make 7.

7 — 4
7 — 3

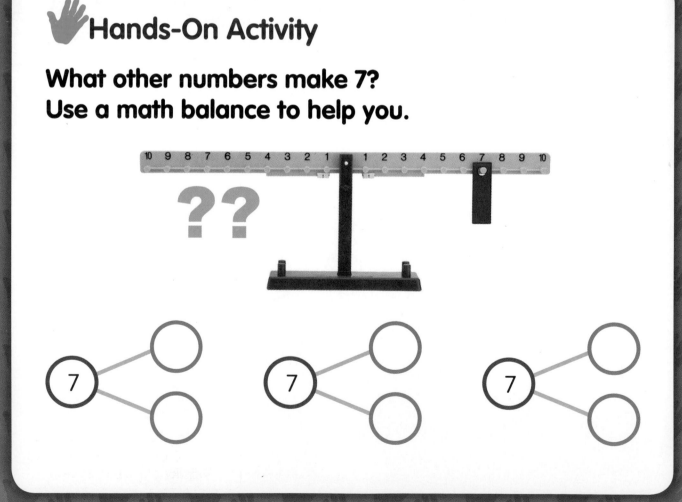

✋ Hands-On Activity

What other numbers make 7?
Use a math balance to help you.

??

7 — ○ ○

7 — ○ ○

7 — ○ ○

Let's Practice

Make number bonds for these numbers.
Use or a math balance to help you.

1

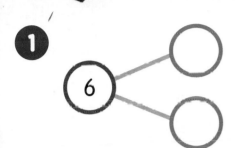

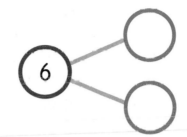

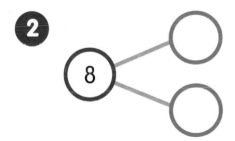

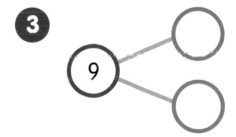

2

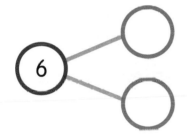

3

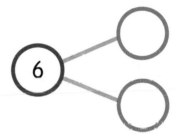

ON YOUR OWN

Go to Workbook A:
Practice 1 to 3, pages 21–30

Math Journal

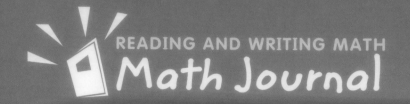

Look at the picture.
Make two number bonds.

red stool and ___ blue stools
make ___ stools.

Let's Explore!

Use 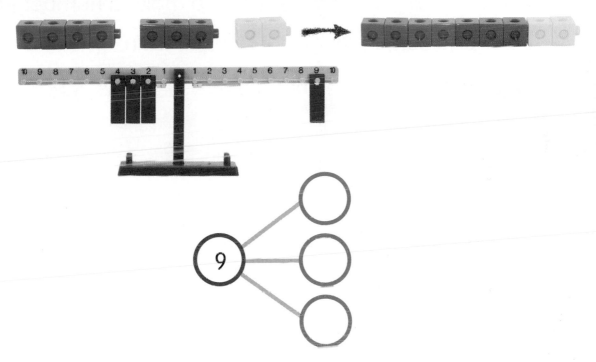 or a math balance to help you.

1 Find three numbers that make 9.

2 Show two more ways to do this.

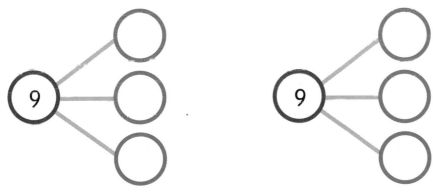

3 Find three numbers that make 10.
Show two more ways to do this.

Let's Explore!

Use  **.**

STEP 1 Put some ▢ and ▢ together to make a number train.

Now add some ▢ to your number train.

Make sure your number train has 10 or less ▢▢.

STEP 2 Count the total number of ▢ and ▢. ▢

Count the number of ▢. ▢

Add the total number of ▢ and ▢ to the number of ▢.

What number do you get? ▢

STEP 3 Count the total number of ▢ and ▢. ▢

Count the number of ▢. ▢

Add the number of ▢ to the total number of ▢ and ▢.

What number do you get? ▢

Did you get the same number for **STEP 2** and **STEP 3** ?

Choose different numbers of ▢, ▢, and ▢.

Carry out **STEP 1**, **STEP 2**, and **STEP 3** again.

What do you notice?

CRITICAL THINKING SKILLS
Put On Your Thinking Cap!

PROBLEM SOLVING
Find the number of beads.
Use number bonds to help you.

1 There are 6 beads under the two cups.

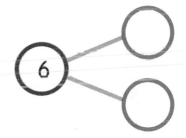

2 There are 8 beads under the two cups.

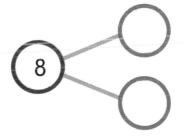

3 There are 10 beads under the three cups.

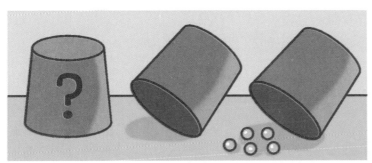

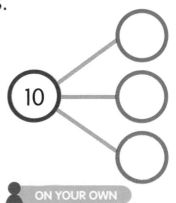

ON YOUR OWN

Go to Workbook A:
Put on Your Thinking Cap!
pages 31–32

Chapter 2 Number Bonds **37**

Chapter Wrap Up

You have learned...

Numbers Bonds

to make a number bond.

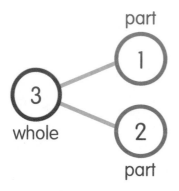

1 and 2 make 3.
1, 2, and 3 make a number bond.

that there are more than one set of parts for a whole.

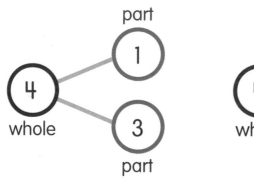

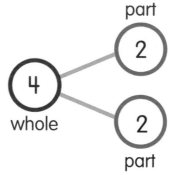

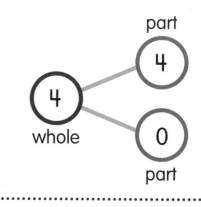

to use a math balance to help you make number bonds.

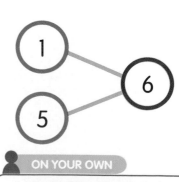

ON YOUR OWN

**Go to Workbook A:
Chapter Review/Test,
pages 33–34**

CHAPTER 3 Addition Facts to 10

I'm riding on the school bus,
On my way to school,
On hops Lou and that makes two.

On goes the school bus,
Down the street, not too fast,
On leaps Sheree and that makes three!

On goes the school bus,
Up the hill, oh so slow!
On jumps Paul and then there are four!

On goes the school bus,
Round the corner, hold on tight!
On climbs Clive and then there are five!

On goes the school bus,
Stopping at the lights,
On plod Sam and Ben and that makes... seven!

Lesson 1 Ways to Add

Lesson 2 Making Addition Stories

Lesson 3 Real-World Problems: Addition

BIG IDEA

Addition can be used to find how many in all.

Counting

There are 6 toys.

| 1 | 2 | 3 | 4 | 5 | 6 |
| one | two | three | four | five | six |

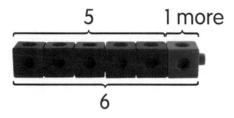

5   1 more

6

1 more than 5 is 6.

Number bonds

There are 6 ribbons in all.

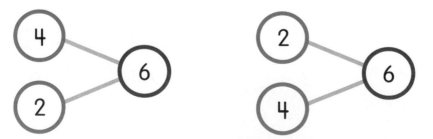

4 red ribbons   2 blue ribbons

4 and 2 make 6.
4, 2, and 6 make a number bond.

Count.

1 1, 2, 3, [____], [____], [____]

2

There are [____] flowers.

1 more than 6 is [____].

3 There are 7 butterflies in all.

[____] white butterflies   [____] black butterflies

Complete the number bonds.

4 5 and 2 make 7.
What other numbers make 7?

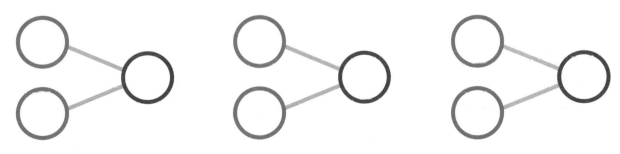

LESSON 1 Ways to Add

Vocabulary
add
plus (+)
equal to (=)
addition sentence
more than
counting tape

Lesson Objectives

• Count on to add.

• Use number bonds to add in any order.

• Write and solve addition sentences.

Learn You can add by counting on.

6 marbles

2 marbles

Add by counting on from the greater number.
6, 7, 8

$$6 + 2 = 8$$
part part whole

+ is read as **plus**.
It means **add**.
= means **equal to**.

You add the parts to find the whole.

6 + 2 = 8 is an **addition sentence**.

Read it as, "Six plus two is **equal to** eight."

Guided Learning

Find the missing numbers.
Count on from the greater number.

1 2 + 5 = ?

5, _____ , _____

2 7 + 3 = ?

7, _____ , _____ , _____

🖐 Hands-On Activity

Use  .

Make the number trains.
Count on from the greater number.
Complete the addition sentence.

1 8

2

_____ , _____ , _____

_____ + _____ = _____

2 4

5

5, _____ , _____ , _____ , _____

4 + 5 = _____

**Count on from the greater number.
Complete the addition sentence.**

 3

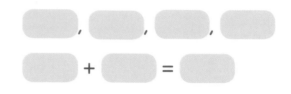

Learn **You can count on to find how many more.**

What is 2 **more than** 7?

> **More than** means
> **added on to.**

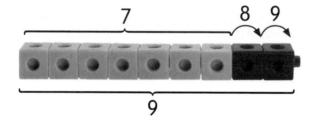

7, 8, 9

9 is 2 more than 7.

2 added on to
7 is 9.

Learn You can count on using a **counting tape**.

Find 2 more than 5.

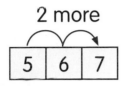

2 more

| 5 | 6 | 7 |

2 more than 5 is 7.

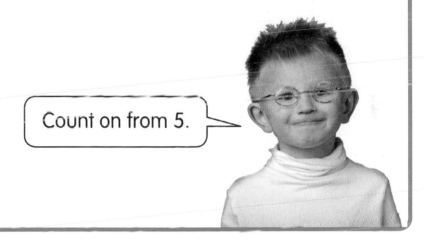

Count on from 5.

Guided Learning

Find the missing numbers.

4 What is 3 more than 5?

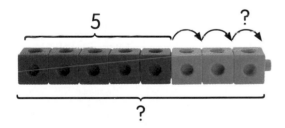

5

?

?

5, ____, ____, ____

____ is 3 more than 5.

5 What is 2 more than 6?

6, ____, ____

[____] is 2 more than 6.

6 What is 3 more than 4?

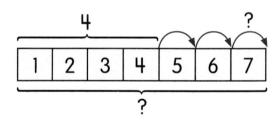

4, ____, ____, ____

[____] is 3 more than 4.

WORKING TOGETHER **Game**

Card Fun!

How to play:

STEP 1 Make two packs of cards.

Pack X
| 1 | 2 | 3 | 0 |
| 1 | 2 | 3 |

Pack Y
| 1 | 2 | 3 | 4 | 5 |
| 6 | 7 |

STEP 2 Player 2 picks a card from Pack X.

STEP 3 Player 2 picks a card from Pack Y.

Players: 3

You need:
• 2 packs of cards

STEP 4 Player 3 adds the numbers on the cards, then says the answer.

STEP 5 Players 1 and 2 check the answer.

STEP 6 Player 3 gets one point if the answer is correct. Take turns to pick cards and add.

After six rounds, the player with the most points wins!

Let's Practice

Add.
Count on from the greater number.

1 $\boxed{4}$ + $\boxed{2}$ =

2 $\boxed{6}$ + $\boxed{1}$ =

3 $\boxed{2}$ + $\boxed{3}$ =

4 $\boxed{7}$ + $\boxed{3}$ =

5 $\boxed{3}$ + $\boxed{5}$ =

6 $\boxed{2}$ + $\boxed{8}$ =

7 What is 4 more than 5?

8 What is 3 more than 6?

9 What is 2 more than 7?

ON YOUR OWN

Go to Workbook A:
Practice 1, pages 41–46

Number bonds can help you add.

How many toy cars are there in all?

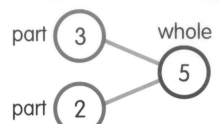 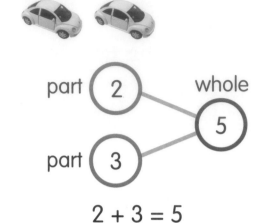

part (3)   whole

(5)

part (2)

$$3 + 2 = 5$$

part (2)   whole

(5)

part (3)

$$2 + 3 = 5$$

There are 5 toy cars in all.

You can add in any order.

$$3 + 2 = 2 + 3$$

Guided Learning

Add. Use number bonds to help you.

6 How many paper clips are there in all?

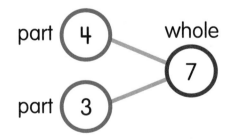

part (4)   whole

(7)

part (3)

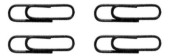 +  =

part (3)   whole

(7)

part (4)

＿ + ＿ = ＿

There are ＿ paper clips in all.

$$4 + 3 = ＿ + ＿$$

Number bonds can help you add.

How many lemons are there in all?

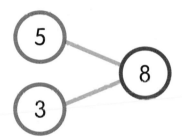

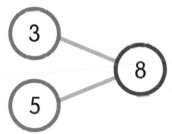

$5 + 3 = 8$

$3 + 5 = 8$

There are 8 lemons in all.

You can add in any order.

$5 + 3 = 3 + 5$

3 added on to 5 is equal to 8.
⬜ added on to ⬜ is also equal to 8.

Add.
Use number bonds to help you.

7 How many monkeys are there in all?

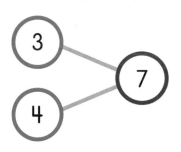 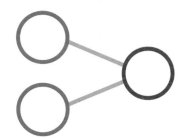

There are ⬜ monkeys in all.

You can add in any order.

4 added on to 3 is equal to 7.
⬜ added on to ⬜ is also equal to 7.

Hands-On Activity

Use and two .

Show 2 + 8.

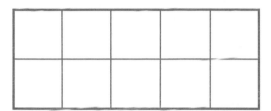

Show 8 + 2.

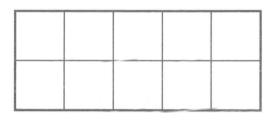

What can you say about 2 + 8 and 8 + 2?

Let's Practice

Complete the number bonds.

1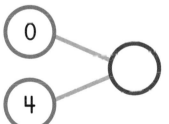

0
4

4
0

2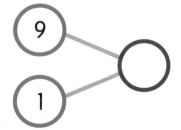

9
1

1
10

Complete the number bonds.
Find the missing numbers.

3 How many crayons are there in all?

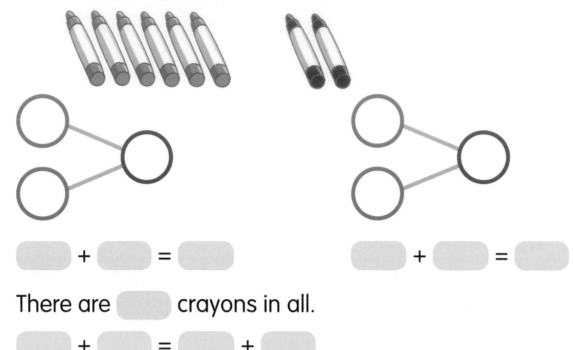

[   ] + [   ] = [   ]   [   ] + [   ] = [   ]

There are [   ] crayons in all.

[   ] + [   ] = [   ] + [   ]

4 How many bees are there in all?

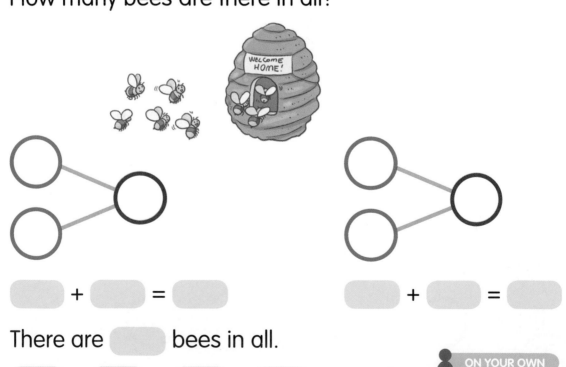

WELCOME HOME!

[   ] + [   ] = [   ]   [   ] + [   ] = [   ]

There are [   ] bees in all.

[   ] + [   ] = [   ] + [   ]

ON YOUR OWN

Go to Workbook A:
Practice 2, pages 47–52

LESSON 2 Making Addition Stories

Lesson Objectives

- Tell addition stories about pictures.
- Write addition sentences.

Learn — You can tell **addition stories** about a picture.

5  are in a pond.

4 🦆 join them.

5 + 4 = 9

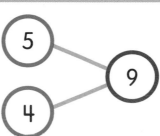

There are 9 🦆 in all.

Guided Learning

Look at the pictures.
Tell an addition story.

big teddy bears

small teddy bears

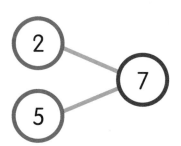

⬜ big teddy bears are on the table.

⬜ small teddy bears are on the table.

$$2 + 5 = 7$$

There are ⬜ teddy bears in all.

2

2 apples

0 apples

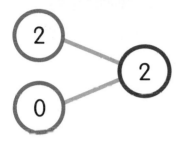

2 + _____ = 2

One plate has _____ apples.

The other plate has _____ apples.

There are _____ apples in all.

3

3 + 1 = _____

_____ girls are playing.

_____ girl joins them.

There are _____ girls in all.

Let's Practice

Look at the picture.
Tell an addition story about each thing.

1 the birds

2 the bicycles

3 the turtles

ON YOUR OWN

Go to Workbook A:
Practice 3, pages 53–56

3 Real-World Problems: Addition

Lesson Objectives

- Write addition sentences.
- Solve real-world problems.

Learn **Read and understand a word problem.**

6 girls are playing.
3 boys are playing with them.
How many children are playing in all?

6 + 3 = 9 ··················

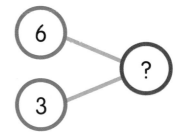

9 children are playing in all.

Guided Learning

Solve.

1 John has 2 baseball cards.
He has 4 football cards.
How many cards does John have in all?

 + =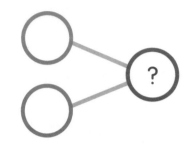

John has [ ] cards in all.

Learn — Read and understand a word problem.

Nick has 4 clay kittens.
He makes 5 more clay kittens.

How many clay kittens does he have now?

4 + 5 = 9 ....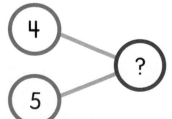

Nick has 9 clay kittens now.

Guided Learning

Solve.

 2

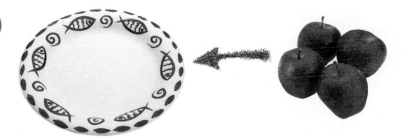

Mary has no apples on her plate.
Tara puts 4 apples on Mary's plate.
How many apples does Mary have now?

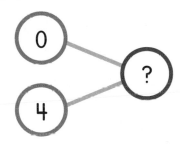

Mary has ▢ apples now.

Let's Practice

Solve.

1 Megan has 4 red markers.
She has 3 blue markers.
How many markers does she have in all?

2 2 children are dancing.
7 children join them.
How many children are dancing now?

3

Jar A

Jar B

Jar A has 5 marbles.
Jar B has 0 marbles.
How many marbles are there in all?

ON YOUR OWN

Go to Workbook A:
Practice 4, pages 57–58

Put On Your Thinking Cap!

PROBLEM SOLVING

Find the missing numbers.

Fill in the ⬜ with 1, 2, 3, 4, 6, or 7.

Use each number once.

Then find the missing number in ⬜, ⬜, and ⬜.

The numbers may be 10 or less than 10.

The answer in ⬜ is to be greater than the answer in ⬜.

The answer in ⬜ is to be less than the answer in ⬜.

⬜ + ⬜ = ⬜

⬜ + ⬜ = ⬜

⬜ + ⬜ = ⬜

There is more than one correct answer.

ON YOUR OWN

Go to Workbook A:
Put on Your Thinking Cap!
pages 59–60

Chapter Wrap Up

You have learned...

Addition Facts to 10

Ways to Add

Count on from the greater number

2 + 3 = ?

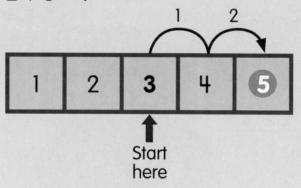

Start here

Tell addition stories about a picture and write an addition sentence for each story.

There is 1 yellow bean.
There are 2 green beans.

1 + 2 = 3

There are 3 beans in all.

Number Bonds

3 + 5 = 8   5 + 3 = 8

3

8

5

5

8

3

You can add in any order.

3 + 5 = 5 + 3

Solve real-world problems

Kelly has 6 stickers.
Her friend gives her 2 stickers.
How many stickers does Kelly have now?

6

8

6 + 2 = 8

2

Kelly has 8 stickers now.

ON YOUR OWN

Go to Workbook A:
Chapter Review/Test,
pages 61–64

Subtraction Facts to 10

BIG IDEA

Subtraction can be used to find how many are left.

Recall Prior Knowledge

Counting

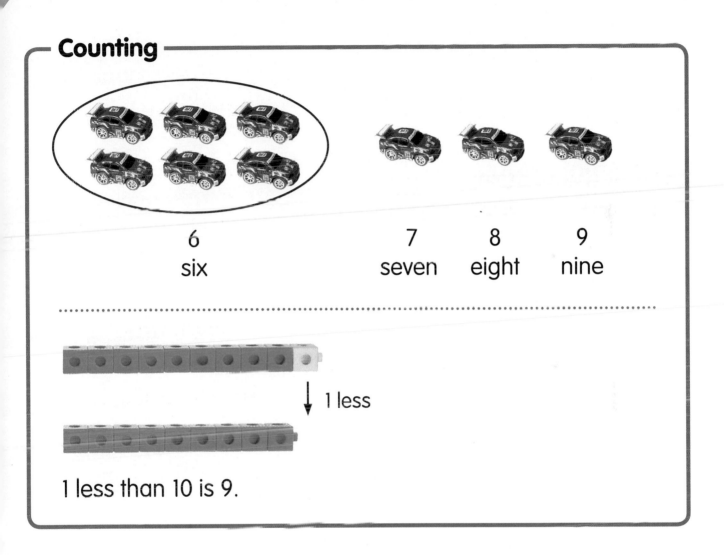

6
six

7
seven

8
eight

9
nine

↓ 1 less

1 less than 10 is 9.

Number bonds

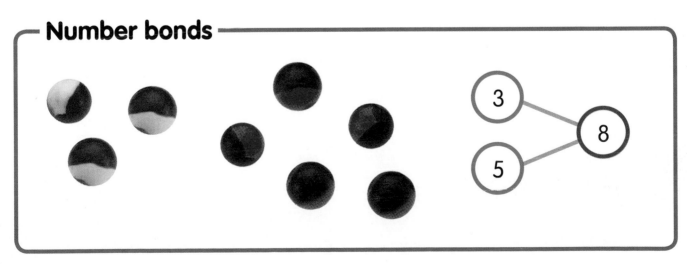

Find the missing numbers in each pattern.

1 2, 3, 4, ____, ____, ____

2 9, 8, 7, ____, ____, ____

Look at the picture.
Complete the number bond.

3

Solve.

4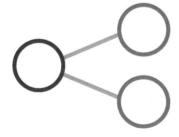

____ is 1 less than 7.

LESSON
1 Ways to Subtract

Lesson Objectives

- Take away to subtract.
- Count on to subtract.
- Count back to subtract.
- Use number bonds to subtract.
- Write and solve subtraction sentences.

Learn **You can subtract by taking away.**

9 spiders are having breakfast.
6 spiders walk away.
How many spiders are left?

Crossing out 6 spiders **takes away** 6 spiders.

You subtract one part from the whole to find the other part.

$$9 - 6 = 3$$

whole part part

− is read as **minus**.
It means **subtract**.

3 spiders are left.

$9 - 6 = 3$ is a **subtraction sentence**.

Read it as, "Nine minus six is equal to three."

Guided Learning

Find how many are left.

1

$10 - 4 = \boxed{}$

2

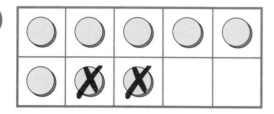

$8 - 2 = \boxed{}$

 # Hands-On Activity

Use ⬤◯ **and** ⬚⬚⬚⬚⬚ .

1 $9 - 3 = ?$
Put 9 ⬤◯ on the ⬚⬚⬚⬚⬚ .
Then take away 3 ⬤◯ .
$9 - 3 = \boxed{}$

Solve.

2 $10 - 5 = \boxed{}$ **3** $8 - 7 = \boxed{}$

Learn

You can take away to find how many less.

What is 2 less than 6?

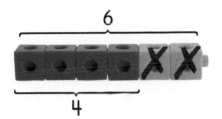

6

4

$6 - 2 = 4$

4 is 2 less than 6.

2 taken away from 6 is 4.

Less than means taken away from.

Guided Learning

Solve.

3 What is 5 less than 8?

8

?

$8 - 5 = $

____ is 5 less than 8.

4 What is 3 less than 7?

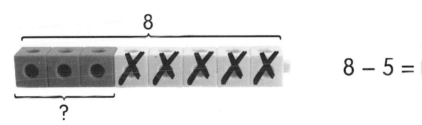

$7 - 3 = $

____ is 3 less than 7.

You can count on to subtract.

9 birds are on a wire.
6 birds fly away.
How many birds are still on the wire?

Find 9 − 6.
Count on from the number that is less, 6.
Stop at 9.

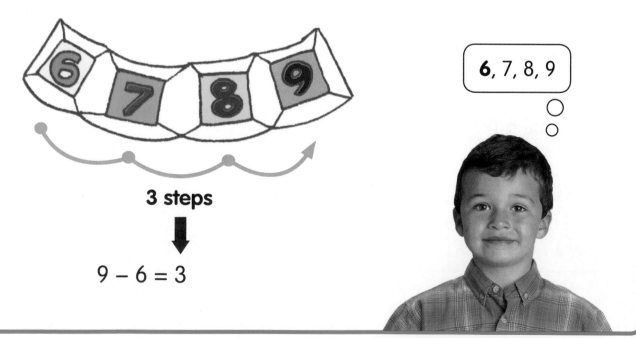

6, 7, 8, 9

3 steps

⬇

9 − 6 = 3

What's Hidden?

Players: 3-4
You need:

How to play:

 STEP 1 Player 1 chooses a number of and shows them to the other players.

STEP 2 Player 1 hides some of them.

STEP 3 The other players must tell the number of Player 1 hid. Count on to find out.

There were 8.

Now there are 5.

5, 6, 7, 8 You hid 3 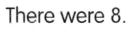!

STEP 4 Check their answer. Take turns to play!

Correct!

Guided Learning

Count on from the number that is less to subtract.
Use the counting tape.

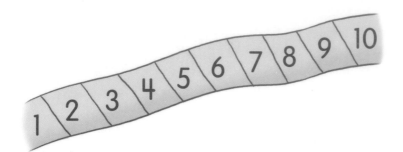

5 8 − 6 = ⬚ **6** 6 − 3 = ⬚

7 10 − 7 = ⬚ **8** 9 − 5 = ⬚

Learn **You can use a counting tape to count back to subtract.**

Find 9 − 2.
Start from the greater number, 9.
Count back 2 steps.

2 steps
↓
9 − 2 = 7

9, 8, 7

Guided Learning

Count back from the greater number to subtract.

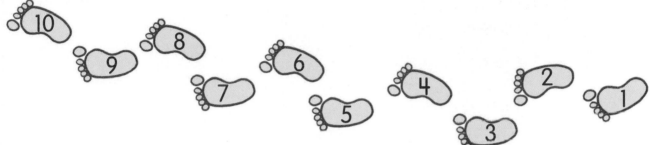

9   7 − 2 = ⬜   **10**   9 − 3 = ⬜

11   8 − 4 = ⬜   **12**   10 − 3 = ⬜

Let's Practice

Solve.

1   What is 3 less than 5? ⬜

2   What is 4 less than 10? ⬜

Count on from the number that is less to subtract.

3   5 − 3 = ⬜   **4**   7 − 3 = ⬜

5   10 − 6 = ⬜   **6**   9 − 4 = ⬜

Count back from the greater number to subtract.

7   9 − 6 = ⬜   **8**   7 − 4 = ⬜

9   8 − 6 = ⬜   **10**   10 − 9 = ⬜

ON YOUR OWN

Go to Workbook A:
Practice 1, pages 65–70

Learn — You can use number bonds to help you subtract.

How many beanbags are on the floor?

$9 - 5 = ?$

part

5

9
whole

4

part

$9 - 5 = 4$

There are 4 beanbags on the floor.

Guided Learning

Use number bonds to subtract.

13 How many yellow beans are there?

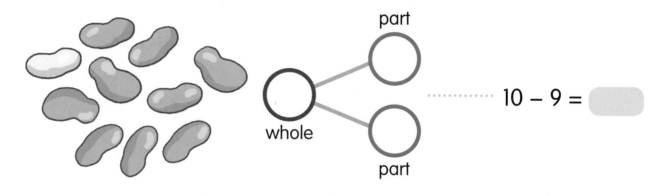

part

whole

part

$10 - 9 = $ ▢

There is ▢ yellow bean.

You can use number bonds to help you subtract.

How many strawberries are left on the plate?

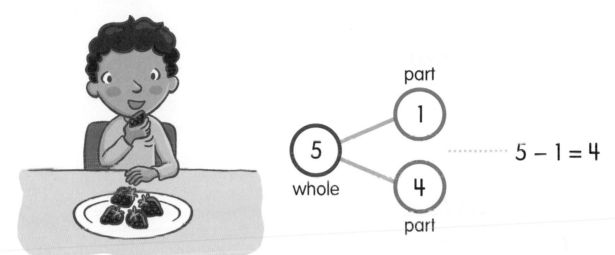

part

1

5 .... 5 − 1 = 4

whole

4

part

4 strawberries are left on the plate.

Guided Learning

Use number bonds to subtract.

14 How many seahorses do not swim away?

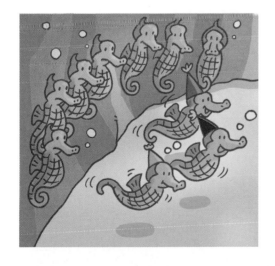

part

○

whole

○

part

10 − ⬭ = ⬭

⬭ seahorses do not swim away.

Let's Practice

Fill in the number bonds.
Complete the subtraction sentences.

1 How many frogs are on a lily pad?

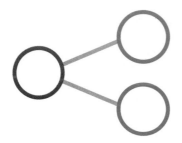 .... 8 – [   ] = [   ]

[   ] frogs are on a lily pad.

2 How many birds are left in the nest?

 .... 9 – [   ] = [   ]

[   ] birds are left in the nest.

ON YOUR OWN

Go to Workbook A:
Practice 2, pages 71–76

Making Subtraction Stories

Lesson Objectives

- Tell subtraction stories about pictures.
- Write subtraction sentences.

Vocabulary
subtraction story

Learn

You can tell subtraction stories about a picture.

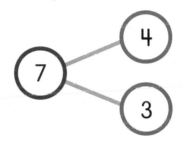

There are 7 animals.
4 are squirrels.

$7 - 4 = 3$

3 are hamsters.

Guided Learning

Look at the picture.
Tell a subtraction story.
Complete the subtraction sentence.

1

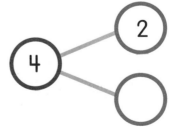

$4 - = $

Learn — You can tell subtraction stories about a picture.

Sarah has 10 apples.
Josh takes 2 apples
from Sarah.

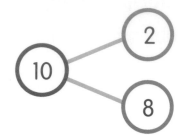

$10 - 2 = 8$

Sarah has 8 apples left.

Guided Learning

Look at the pictures.
Tell a subtraction story.
Complete the subtraction sentence.

$8 - \quad = \quad$

 Hands-On Activity

Use ●●.

1 Put some counters on the table.
Then take away 0 counters.
How many counters are left on the table?

◯ – 0 = ◯

2 Try this again.
Put a different number of counters on the table.
Then take away 0 counters.
How many counters are left on the table?

◯ – 0 = ◯

What do you notice?

3 Tell a story about taking away 0.

Example

I have 3 buttons on my jeans.
0 buttons fall off.
3 – 0 = 3

Make a subtraction sentence for each picture.

1

2

Look at the picture.
Tell subtraction stories about it.
Make a subtraction sentence for each story.

3

ON YOUR OWN

Go to Workbook A:
Practice 3, pages 77–80

LESSON 3 Real-World Problems: Subtraction

Lesson Objectives

• Write subtraction sentences.

• Solve real-world word problems.

Learn **Read and understand a word problem.**

Nora and Keisha have 9 oranges.
Nora has 7 oranges.
How many oranges does Keisha have?

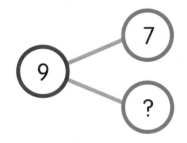

$9 - 7 = 2$

Keisha has 2 oranges.

Guided Learning

Solve.

1 There are 8 ants.
   3 ants are black.
   How many ants are red?

▢ – ▢ = ▢

▢ ants are red.

Subtract to solve word problems by taking away.

There are 10 biscuits on a plate.
Luis takes some.
6 biscuits are left.
How many biscuits does he take?

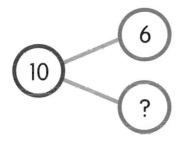

$$10 - 6 = 4$$

Luis takes 4 biscuits.

Guided Learning

Solve.

2 Jackie has 9 balloons.
2 balloons burst.
How many balloons does
Jackie have left?

 =

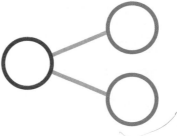

Jackie has ⬭ balloons left.

Solve.

A tree has 7 lemons.
2 of the lemons are yellow.
How many lemons are green?

There are 10 muffins.
Hector takes some.
3 muffins are left.
How many muffins does Hector take?

ON YOUR OWN

Go to Workbook A:
Practice 4, pages 81–82

LESSON 4 Making Fact Families

Lesson Objectives

- Recognize related addition and subtraction sentences.
- Write fact families.
- Use fact families to solve real-world problems.
- Determine if number sentences involving addition and subtraction are true or false.

Learn Addition and subtraction are related.

How many balls of wool are yellow?

$7 - 2 = 5$

How many balls of wool are blue?

$7 - 5 = 2$

How many balls of wool are there in all?

$2 + 5 = 7$ or $5 + 2 = 7$

$7 - 2 = 5$ $\qquad$ $7 - 5 = 2$ $\qquad$ $2 + 5 = 7$ $\qquad$ $5 + 2 = 7$

This is a **fact family**.

Each fact in a fact family has the same parts and whole.

Guided Learning

Look at the picture.
Find the missing numbers in the fact family.

1

$4 + 2 = 6$ $6 - 4 = 2$

[ ] + [ ] = [ ]   [ ] − [ ] = [ ]

Make a fact family for each picture.

2

[ ] + [ ] = [ ]

[ ] + [ ] = [ ]

[ ] − [ ] = [ ]

[ ] − [ ] = [ ]

3

[ ] + [ ] = [ ]

[ ] + [ ] = [ ]

[ ] − [ ] = [ ]

[ ] − [ ] = [ ]

You can use related addition facts to solve subtraction sentences.

Sandra has some .
She puts 5 in a bag.
3 are left.
How many did Sandra have?

☐ − 5 = 3

5 + 3 = 8 is the related addition fact.
So, 8 − 5 = 3.
Sandra had 8 .

| 5 + 3 = 8 |

Guided Learning

Solve.

4 Sal has some granola bars.
He gives 4 to his brother.
Sal has 5 left.
How many granola bars did Sal have?

 − 4 = 5

4 + 5 = ☐ is the related addition fact.

So, ☐ − 4 = 5

Sal had ☐ granola bars.

Learn You can use related subtraction facts to solve addition sentences.

Terrel has 3 pencils.
Joe gives him some pencils.
Terrel now has 7 pencils.
How many pencils does Joe give Terrel?

3 + ⬜ = 7

$7 - 3 = 4$

$7 - 3 = 4$ is the related subtraction fact.
So, 3 + 4 = 7.
Joe gives Terrel 4 pencils.

Guided Learning

Solve.

5 Jasmine has 6 ladybugs in a jar.
She finds some ladybugs in the garden.
Jasmine now has 10 ladybugs.
How many ladybugs does she find?

6 + ⬜ = 10

10 − 6 = ⬜ is the related subtraction fact.

So, 6 + ⬜ = 10.

Jasmine finds ⬜ ladybugs.

You can find out if a number sentence is true or false.

We can say 7 + 2 = 9 and 9 − 2 = 7.
These number sentences are **true**.

Can we say 7 + 2 = 8? No.
What about 9 − 2 = 5? No.
So, these number sentences are **false**.

7 + 2 = 9   2 + 7 = 9

Both number sentences have the same parts and whole.
So, we can say 7 + 2 = 2 + 7.
This number sentence is true.

Is 7 + 2 = 4 + 3 a true number sentence?

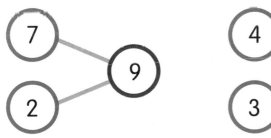

7 + 2 = 9   4 + 3 = 7

No, the number sentence does not have the same parts and whole.
9 is not equal to 7.
So, this number sentence is false.

Guided Learning

Complete.

1 Is 5 + 3 = 9 a true number sentence?

5 + 3 =

Is the same as 9?

So, this number sentence is . (true or false)

2 Is 4 = 10 − 6 a true number sentence?

10 − 6 =

Is the same as 4?

So, this number sentence is . (true or false)

Let's Practice

Use the pictures to write a fact family.

1

Use the numbers to write a fact family.

2 10 2 8

Find the missing number.
Use related facts to help you.

3 $2 +$ ▢ $= 7$

4 $6 +$ ▢ $= 9$

5 $7 -$ ▢ $= 3$

6 $10 -$ ▢ $= 4$

7 ▢ $+ 3 = 5$

8 ▢ $+ 5 = 8$

9 ▢ $- 4 = 4$

10 ▢ $- 6 = 3$

Is the number sentence true or false?
Circle the correct answer.

11 $5 - 4 = 9$ true   false

12 $8 + 4 = 4$ true   false

13 $9 - 5 = 4$ true   false

14 $8 - 6 = 3$ true   false

15 $4 + 1 = 1 + 3$ true   false

16 $6 + 2 = 2 + 6$ true   false

17 $4 + 5 = 5 + 4$ true   false

ON YOUR OWN

Go to Workbook A:
Practice 5, pages 83–86

 **Let's Explore!**

Use these cards.

| 2 | 3 | 6 | 8 | 9 | 10 | + | − | = |

Use the cards to make number sentences.
Use each card once in each number sentence.
Write all the number sentences you make.

CRITICAL THINKING SKILLS
Put On Your Thinking Cap!

PROBLEM SOLVING

1 Fill in the ⬤ with these numbers.

(1) (2) (3) (5) (6) (8) (9)

➡ and ⬇ mean =.
Use each number once.

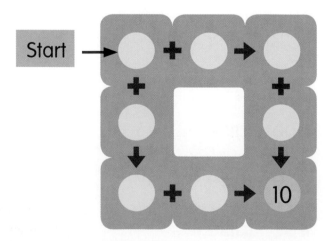

Put On Your Thinking Cap!

PROBLEM SOLVING

2 Fill in the ⬤ with these numbers.

(2) (3) (4) (5) (6) (7) (8)

➜ and ⬇ mean =.
Use each number once.

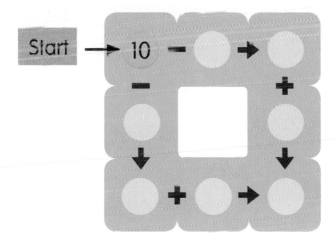

ON YOUR OWN

Go to Workbook A:
Put on Your Thinking Cap!
pages 87–88

Chapter Wrap Up
You have learned...

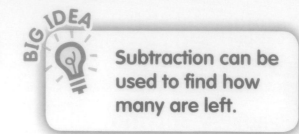

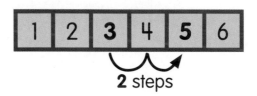
Subtraction Facts to 10

to subtract by taking away.

$3 - 1 = 2$

to subtract by counting on from the number that is less.

$5 - 3 = 2$

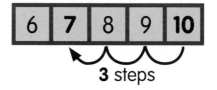
2 steps

to subtract by counting back from the greater number.

$10 - 3 = 7$

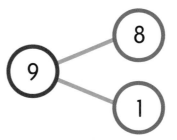
3 steps

to subtract using number bonds.

$9 - 8 = 1$

to tell subtraction stories about pictures and write a subtraction sentence for each story.

There are 3 clay kittens.
2 are yellow.
$3 - 2 = 1$
1 is not yellow.

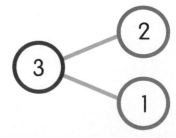

to solve real-world problems.

Mom has 4 eggs.
Anita eats some eggs.
1 egg is left.
How many eggs does Anita eat?
4 – 1 = 3
Anita eats 3 eggs.

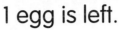

to make a fact family.

$2 + 6 = 8$ $6 + 2 = 8$ $8 - 2 = 6$ $8 - 6 = 2$

Each fact in a fact family has the same parts and whole.

to use fact families to solve real-world problems.

James has 1 sock.
He finds more socks under his bed.
He has 3 socks now.
How many socks does he find?

$1 + \boxed{} = 3$

$3 - 1 = 2$ is the related subtraction fact.

So, $1 + 2 = 3$.
James finds 2 socks under his bed.

to find out if a number sentence is true or false.

$5 + 3 = 8$ is true.

$7 - 3 = 5$ is false.

ON YOUR OWN

Go to Workbook A:
Chapter Review/Test,
pages 89–92

 5 Shapes and Patterns

Once upon a time, there was a place called the Land of Shapes. Many shapes lived there. They worked, played, and ate together.

One day, a strange visitor came. The visitor wanted to live in the Land of Shapes. The shapes looked at the visitor. One shape said, "You are not like us. How can you live here?"

The visitor smiled.
He said, "I am not only one shape, I can be any shape!"
He then turned himself into the different shapes.

The shapes thought this was great!
They decided to let the visitor stay.
So the visitor stayed and they all lived happily ever after.

BIG IDEA

Explore, identify, and compare plane and solid shapes in patterns and in the real world.

Recall Prior Knowledge

These are shapes.

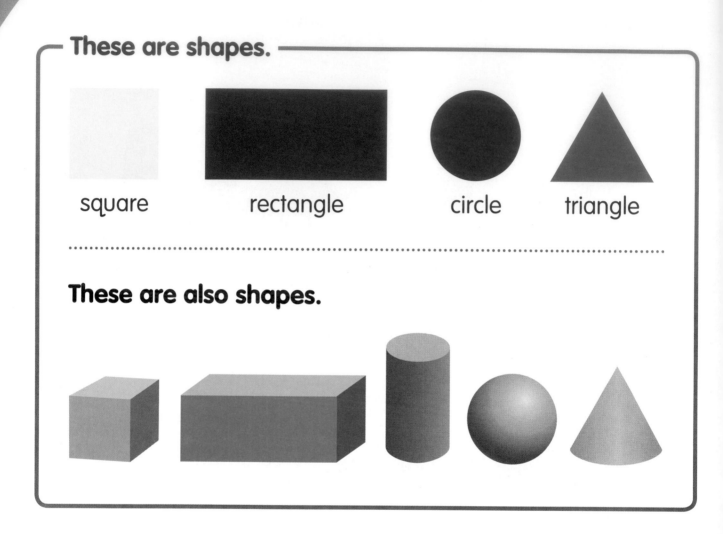

square   rectangle   circle   triangle

These are also shapes.

This is a pattern.

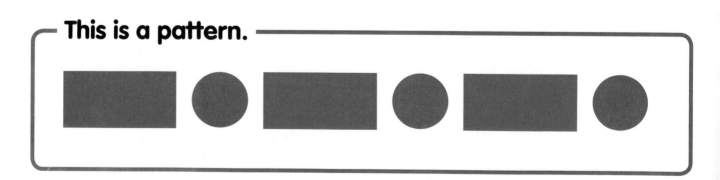

✔ Quick Check

1 Name each shape.

2 Match the shapes to the things.

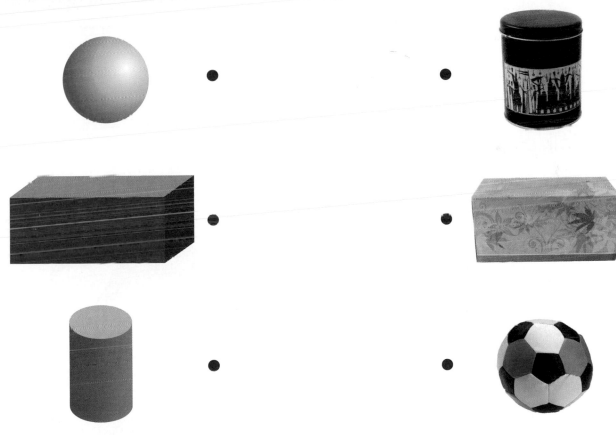

3 Look at the pattern.
Choose the shape that comes next.

LESSON 1

Exploring Plane Shapes

Lesson Objectives

- Identify, classify, and describe plane shapes.
- Divide shapes into two and four equal parts and describe the parts.
- Describe the whole as the sum of its parts.

Learn Get to know shapes.

Trace these shapes with your finger.
Talk about them.

circles

triangles

squares

rectangles

Guided Learning

Find the shapes that are <u>not</u> squares.

1

About sides and corners.

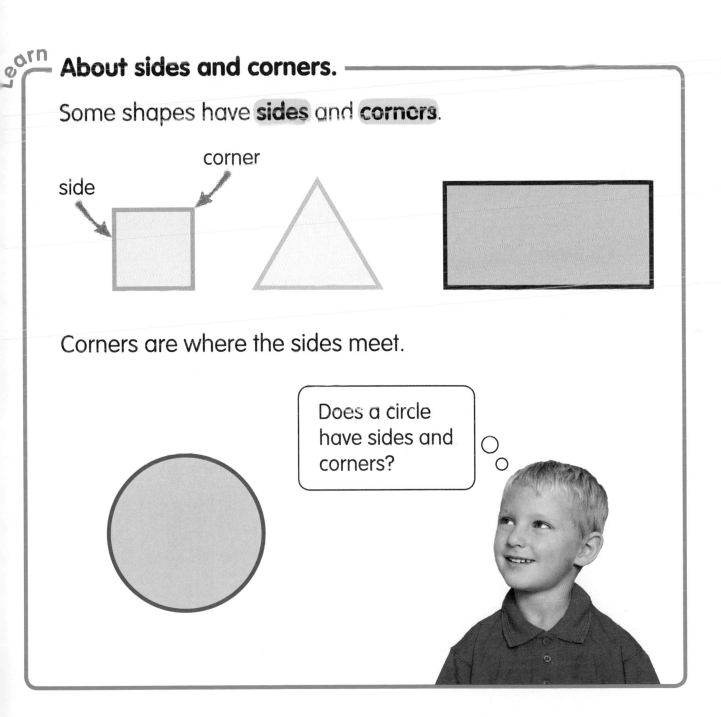

Some shapes have **sides** and **corners**.

corner

side

Corners are where the sides meet.

Does a circle have sides and corners?

Guided Learning

Count the number of sides.
Then count the number of corners.

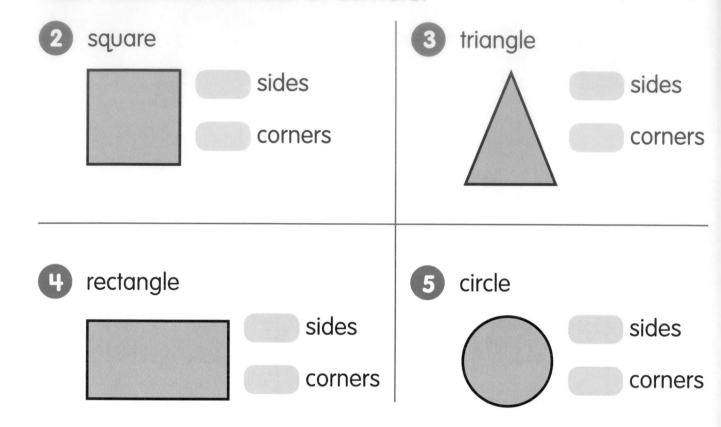

2 square

☐ sides

☐ corners

3 triangle

☐ sides

☐ corners

4 rectangle

☐ sides

☐ corners

5 circle

☐ sides

☐ corners

Learn **You can sort shapes in many ways.**

red

purple

These shapes are the same **color**.
They are **alike**.

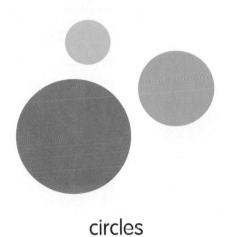

circles

rectangles

These shapes are the same **shape**.

small

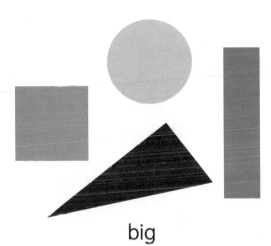

big

These shapes are the same **size**.

3 sides and 3 corners

4 sides and 4 corners

These shapes have the same number of sides and corners.

Guided Learning

Tell how these shapes are alike.

6

Are these shapes alike in another way?

 Learn **Shapes can be alike in some ways and different in other ways.**

How are these shapes alike?

They are triangles.
They are the same size.
They have the same number of sides and corners.

Is their color alike?
No. They are **different** colors.

Guided Learning

Tell how these shapes are different.

Are these shapes different in another way?

7

 Hands-On Activity

Use these.

Sort by:

1 shape   **2** color   **3** size

4 number of sides

5 number of corners

Let's Practice

Find the answers.

1 Find the triangles.
How many triangles are there? ⬭

2 Find the rectangles.
How many rectangles are there? ⬭

Which name does **not** belong?

3

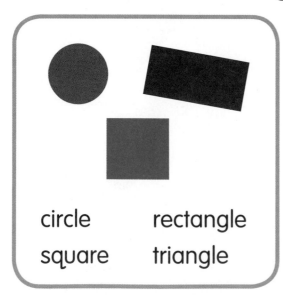

circle	rectangle
square	triangle

4

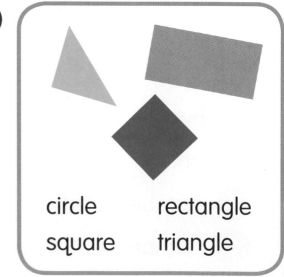

circle	rectangle
square	triangle

Find the answers.

5 Name the shape that has 3 sides and 3 corners.

6 Tell how these shapes are alike.
Tell how they are different.

7 Find the shapes that are of the same size <u>and</u> the same shape.

ON YOUR OWN

**Go to Workbook A:
Practice 1, pages 97–102**

Use folding to make shapes that are alike.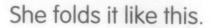

Judy has a piece of paper.
It is the shape of a rectangle.

She folds it like this.

Then, she unfolds it and
draws a line along the fold.

Now she has two shapes
Shape A and Shape B.

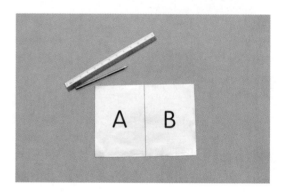

What can you say about the two shapes?

They have the same shape and color.
They have the same size.
They have the same number of sides.
They have the same number of corners.
They are alike.

Shapes A and B
fit exactly over
each other.

Is there anything
different about
the shapes?

Guided Learning

**Look at the pictures.
Solve.**

Judy folds her piece of paper.   She unfolds it.

What can you say about the two shapes?
How are they alike?

✋ Hands-On Activity

1 Fold a square piece of paper to make two shapes that
are alike.

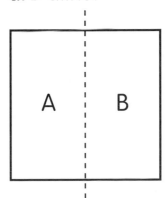

Can you make two
triangles that are
alike using a square
piece of paper?

2 Now fold another piece of paper a different way.
Make two shapes that are alike.

You can divide shapes into equal parts.

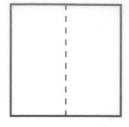

The square is divided into 2 equal parts.
Each part is one **half of** the square.

The 2 equal parts are smaller
than the whole square.

2 equal parts or **2 halves**
make 1 whole.

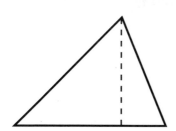

The triangle shows 2 parts.
Does it show halves?

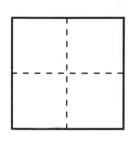

The square is divided into 4 equal parts.
Each part is one **fourth of** the square.

You can also say that each part is one **quarter of** the square.

4 equal parts or **4 fourths** or **4 quarters** make 1 whole.

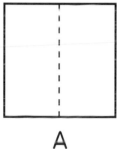

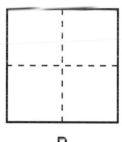

A   B

Which square has smaller parts?

The more equal parts we divide a shape into, the smaller parts we get.

Guided Learning

Check the shapes that show halves.

 9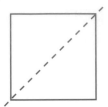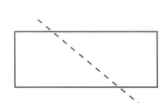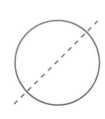

Check the shapes that show fourths.

 10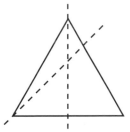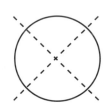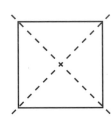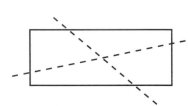

Let's Practice

Color.
Circle the correct answer.

1 Color one part of the circle blue.

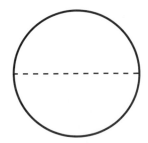

One **half of / fourth of** the circle is blue.

2 Color one part of the square red.

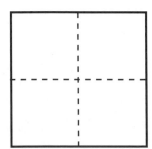

One **half of / fourth of** the square is red.

3 Color 3 quarters of the rectangle yellow.

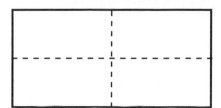

There are two whole pizzas which are cut into equal parts.

Pizza A   Pizza B

4 How many equal parts make up the whole of Pizza A?

5 How many equal parts make up the whole of Pizza B?

6 Which whole pizza is cut into halves?

7 Which whole pizza has more parts?

8 Which whole pizza's parts are bigger?

9 Which is bigger, a half of Pizza A or a fourth of Pizza B?

ON YOUR OWN

Go to Workbook A:
Practice 2, pages 103–106

Exploring Solid Shapes

LESSON 2

Lesson Objective

• Identify, classify, and sort solid shapes.

Learn

Get to know solid shapes.

Trace these solid shapes with your finger.
Talk about them.

rectangular prism

cube

sphere

cone

cylinder

pyramid

Name and compare solid shapes.

These are rectangular prisms.

These are cubes.

These are spheres.

These are cones.

These are cylinders.

These are pyramids.

Guided Learning

Find the shapes that are <u>not</u> cubes.

1

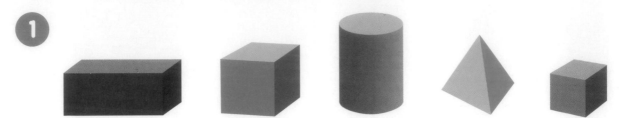

You can move solid shapes in different ways.

You can **stack** and **slide** these shapes.

You can **roll** these shapes.

Hands-On Activity

1 Show your classmate the correct shape.
Can you make the shape stack, slide, or roll?
Make an ✗ in your table if you can.

Solid Shape		Stack	Roll	Slide
rectangular prism				
sphere				
cube				
cylinder				
cone				

Now talk about the shapes.

2 Which shapes can you stack?

3 Which shapes can you roll?

4 Which shapes can you <u>not</u> slide?

5 Which two shapes can be moved in the same ways?

6 Is there a shape that you can stack, roll, and slide?

Let's Practice

1 Find the cubes.

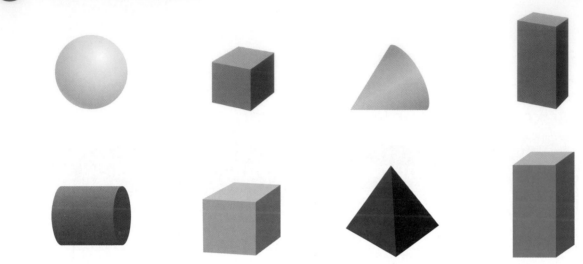

Name each solid shape.

2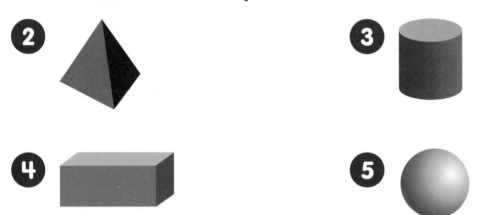

3

4

5

Look around you.
Find two things that look like these solid shapes.

6 cylinder

7 cone

Sort the solid shapes.

8 Find the shapes that can stack.

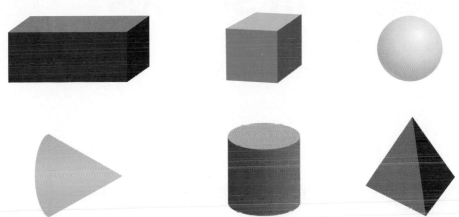

9 Find the shapes that can roll.

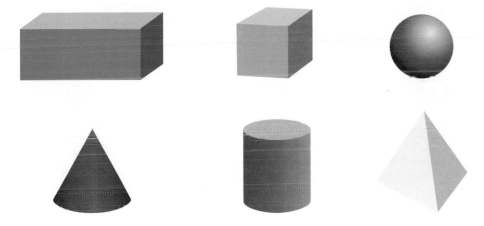

10 Find the shapes that can slide.

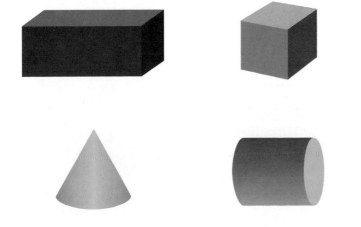

ON YOUR OWN

Go to Workbook A:
Practice 3, pages 107–110

LESSON 3 Making Pictures and Models with Shapes

Lesson Objective

• Combine and separate plane and solid shapes.

Learn **You can combine plane shapes.**

Here are 2 rectangles, 2 triangles, and a square.

I can make a picture like this.

I can make a picture like this.

Guided Learning

Solve.

1 Name the shapes that make this picture.

Shapes	How many?
triangles	
rectangles	
squares	
circles	

Hands-On Activity

1 Make a picture with these shapes.
How many of each shape are there?

You can use all or
some of the shapes.

Tech Connection

2 Use shapes to make a picture on the computer.

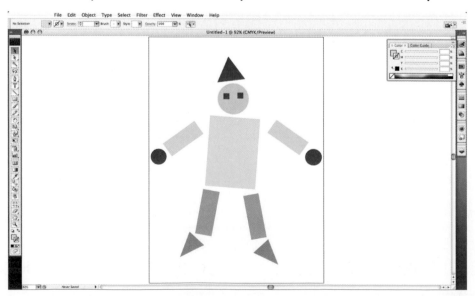

✋ Hands-On Activity

3 Cut out a copy of these shapes.

Put any two of the shapes together to make these shapes.

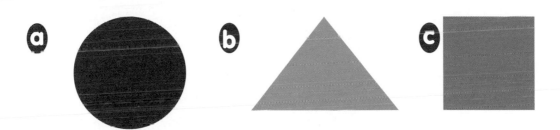

a   **b**   **c**

🔍 Let's Explore!

Use these shapes.

Make two different pictures. Use a copy of all these shapes in each picture.

Let's Practice

Count.
Look at the picture.

1 This picture is made of many shapes.

How many of these shapes can you find?

Shapes	How many?
triangles	
rectangles	
squares	
circles	

ON YOUR OWN

Go to Workbook A:
Practice 4, pages 111–116

Learn

You can build models with solid shapes.

Here is 1 sphere, 2 pyramids, 4 cylinders, 2 cubes, 1 cone, and 1 rectangular prism.

I can make a model like this.

I can make a model like this.

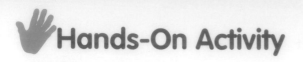

Hands-On Activity

Use .

Make your own model.
Find the number of each solid shape in your model.

Solid		How many?
cube		
sphere		
rectangular prism		
pyramid		
cylinder		
cone		

Guided Learning

Look at the model.
Find the number of each solid shape in the model.

2

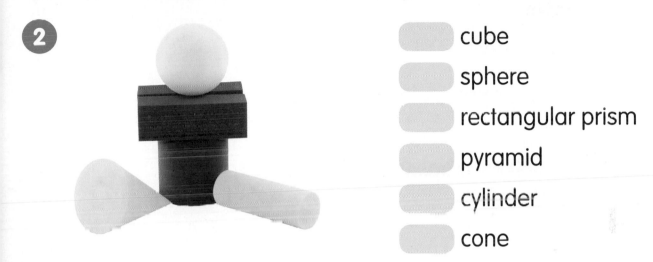

	cube
	sphere
	rectangular prism
	pyramid
	cylinder
	cone

Let's Practice

Look at the model.
Find the number of each solid shape in the model.

1

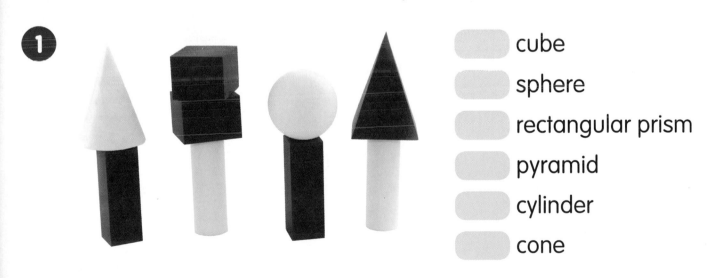

	cube
	sphere
	rectangular prism
	pyramid
	cylinder
	cone

ON YOUR OWN

Go to Workbook A:
Practice 5, pages 117–118

LESSON 4 Seeing Shapes Around Us

Lesson Objective

• Identify plane and solid shapes in real life.

Learn

You can see shapes in things around you.

This is a CD.
It has the shape of a circle.

This is an envelope.
It has the shape of a rectangle.

Guided Learning

1 This is a slice of cheese.
It has the shape of a ____ .

Learn

You can see shapes in things around you.

This is a container.
It has the shape of a rectangular prism.

This is a tennis ball.
It has the shape of a sphere.

Guided Learning

2 This is a popcorn tin.
It has the shape of a [　　　].

 **Hands-On Activity**

WORK IN PAIRS

Look around your classroom and school. Find two things that have these shapes.

1 circle [　　　]   **2** rectangle [　　　]

3 square [　　　]   **4** triangle [　　　]

5 sphere [　　　]   **6** rectangular prism [　　　]

7 cube [　　　]

Can you find one thing that has these shapes?

8 cone [　　　]   **9** pyramid [　　　]

Hands-On Activity

Use .

Draw around each shape.
What shape do you make?

1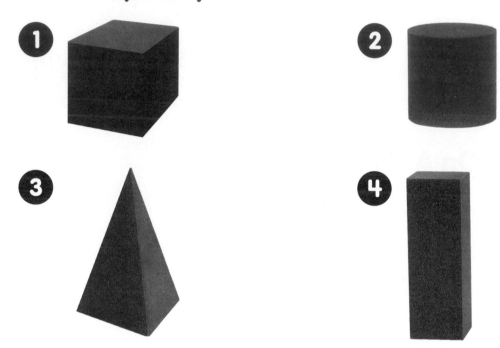

2

3

4

Try turning the pyramid around.
Can you make a different shape?

Let's Practice

Look at the pictures.
Name the shapes you see.

Answer the questions.

5 This is a sponge.
What shape does it have?
What other shapes do you see?

6 This is a sharpener.
What shape does it have?
What other shapes do you see?

Look at the picture.
What solid shapes can you see?
What plane shapes can you see?

7

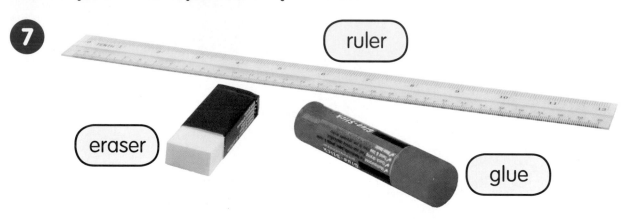

ruler

eraser

glue

8

cereal

Cereal

granola bar

orange

ON YOUR OWN

Go to Workbook A:
Practice 6, pages 119–122

LESSON 5 Making Patterns with Plane Shapes

Lesson Objective

- Use plane shapes to identify, extend, and create patterns.

Vocabulary
repeating pattern

Learn

These are **repeating patterns.**

This pattern repeats.
Circle, triangle,
circle, triangle...

There is a change in shape.

Big, small, big, small...

There is a change in size.

Blue, red, blue, red...

There is a change in color.

Guided Learning

Complete the patterns.

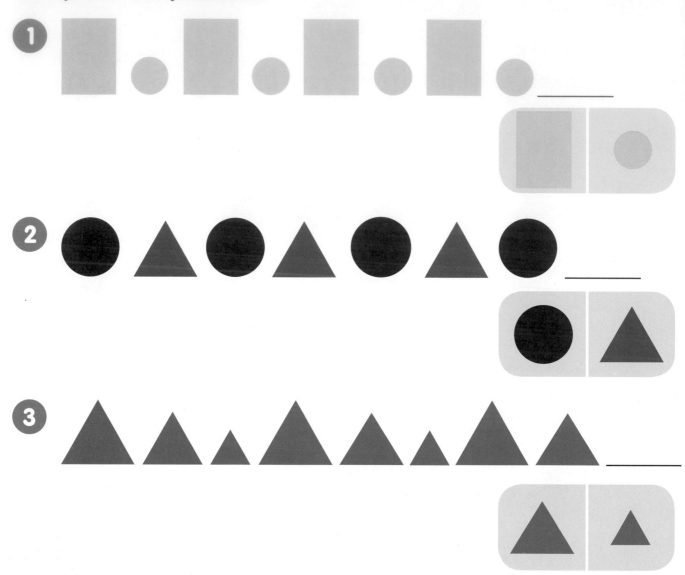

1.

2.

3.

👋 **Hands-On Activity**

Tech Connection

Make a repeating pattern with two shapes on the computer.
Print the pattern you have made.
Ask your classmates what comes next.

Let's Practice

Complete the patterns.

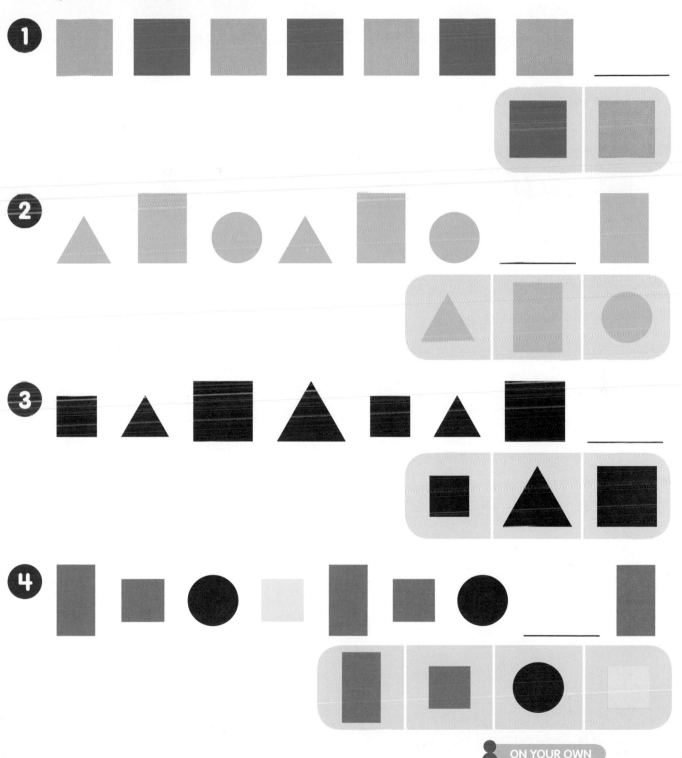

ON YOUR OWN

Go to Workbook A:
Practice 7, pages 123–128

Making Patterns with Solid Shapes

Lesson Objective

• Use solid shapes to identify, extend, and create patterns.

Learn These are more repeating patterns.

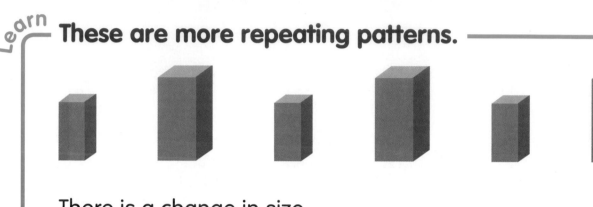

There is a change in size.

There is a change in color.

There is a change in shape.

Guided Learning

Complete the patterns.

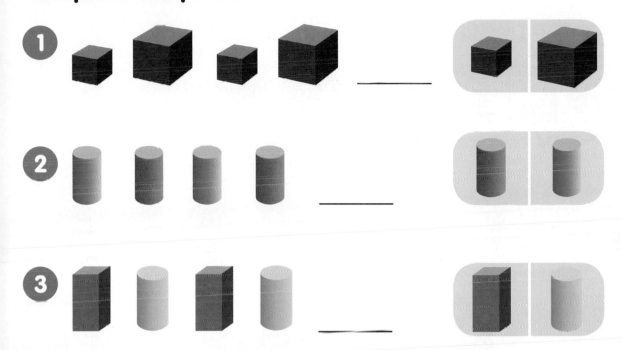

1 _____

2

3

Hands-On Activity

WORK IN PAIRS

Use .

Make your own pattern.
Ask your classmate to show what comes next.

Example

Let's Practice

Complete the patterns.

1  _____ _____

2  _____

3  _____ _____

ON YOUR OWN

**Go to Workbook A:
Practice 8, pages 129–132**

CRITICAL THINKING SKILLS
Put On Your Thinking Cap!

PROBLEM SOLVING

1 How are these shapes sorted?

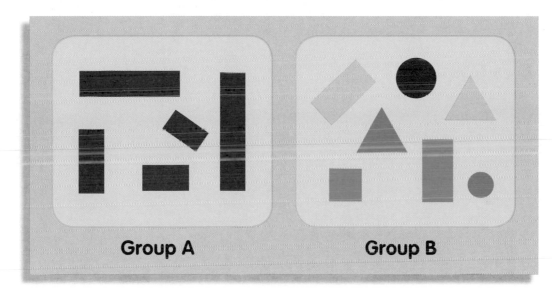

Group A　　　　　　　**Group B**

2 What comes next in this pattern?

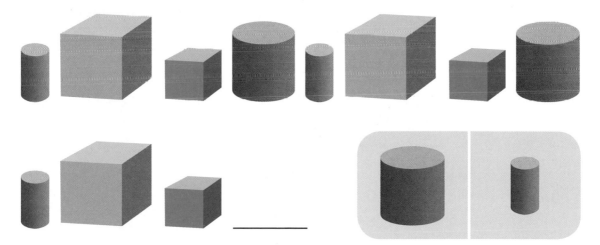

ON YOUR OWN

**Go to Workbook A:
Put on Your Thinking Cap!
pages 133–138**

Chapter Wrap Up

You have learned...

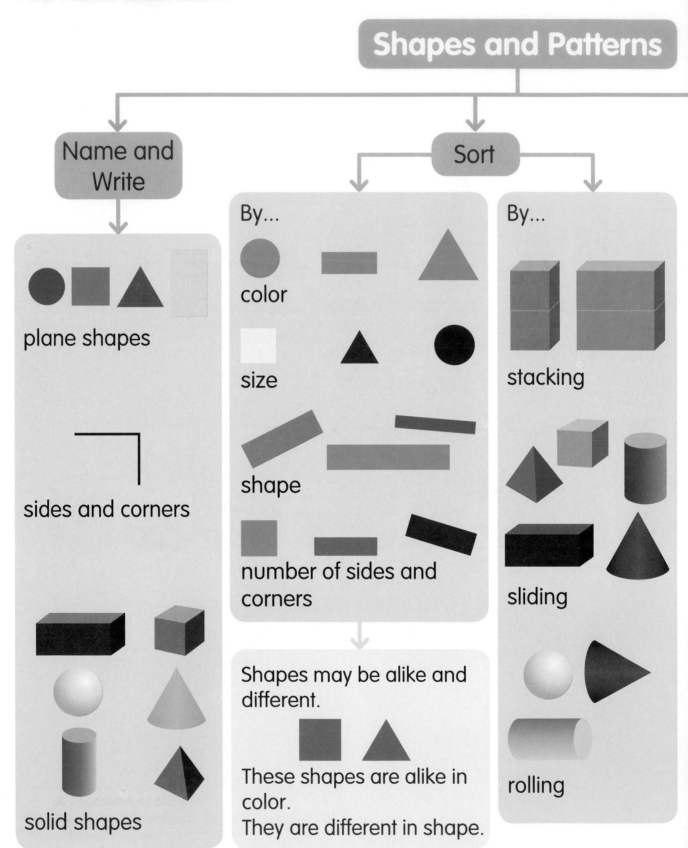

Shapes and Patterns

Name and Write

plane shapes

sides and corners

solid shapes

Sort

By...

color

size

shape

number of sides and corners

Shapes may be alike and different.

These shapes are alike in color.
They are different in shape.

By...

stacking

sliding

rolling

Explore, identify, and compare plane and solid shapes in patterns and in the real world.

Make Pictures and Models

With...

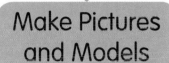

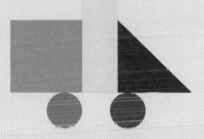

plane shapes

solid shapes

Divide Shapes into Equal Parts

One half of the square is green.

One fourth of the circle Is shaded. Three quarters of the circle is not shaded.

Make Repeating Patterns

There is a change in...

size

shape

color

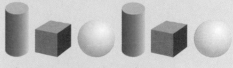

shape and color

ON YOUR OWN

Go to Workbook A:
Chapter Review/Test,
pages 139–142

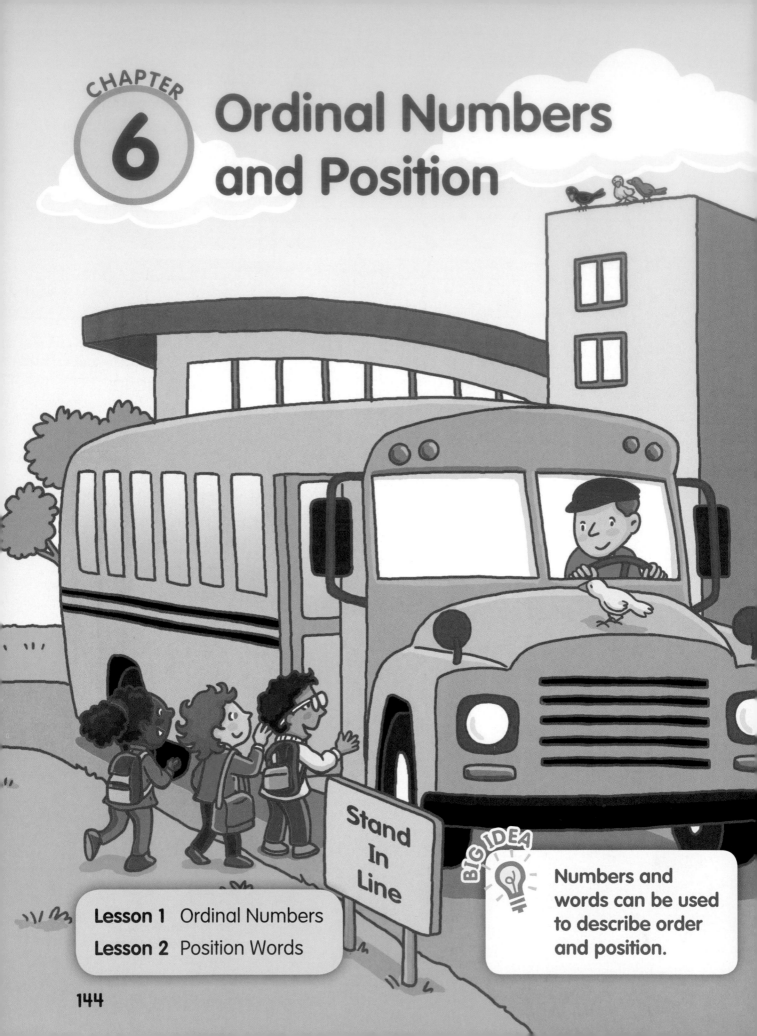

CHAPTER 6 Ordinal Numbers and Position

Lesson 1 Ordinal Numbers
Lesson 2 Position Words

Stand In Line

BIG IDEA
Numbers and words can be used to describe order and position.

Recall Prior Knowledge

Position numbers and words

Carl
3rd
third

Sam
2nd
second

Jackie
1st
first

Jackie is first in line.
Sam is next in line.
Carl is last in line.

✔ Quick Check

1 _____ is second in line.

2 _____ is 3rd in line.

3 _____ is 1st in line.

LESSON 1 Ordinal Numbers

Lesson Objective

• Use ordinal numbers.

Learn You can use ordinal numbers to tell order.

Hippo **3rd** third

Flipper **1st** first

Alice **5th** fifth

Wally **2nd** second

Ben **4th** fourth

Vocabulary

first   second   third   fourth   fifth
sixth   seventh   eighth   ninth   tenth
last

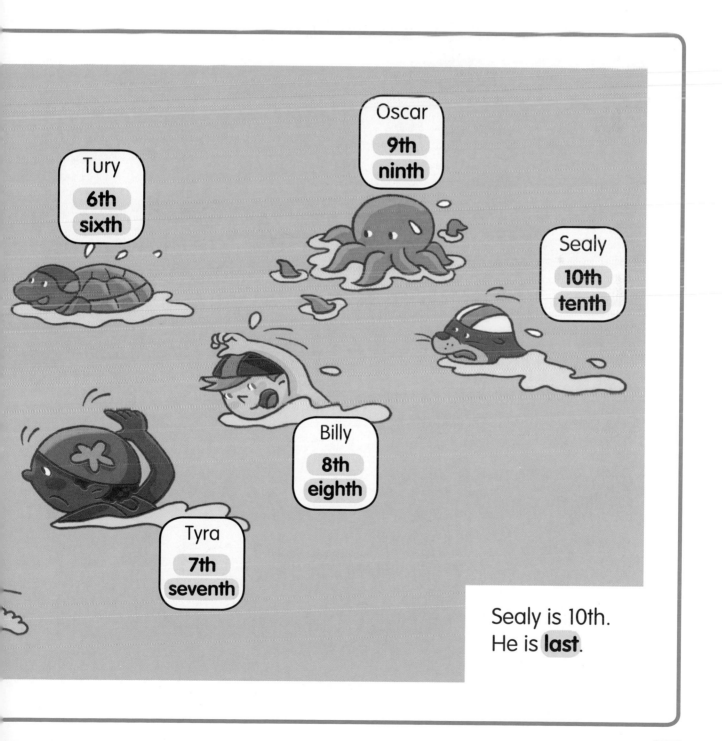

Oscar
9th
ninth

Tury
6th
sixth

Sealy
10th
tenth

Billy
8th
eighth

Tyra
7th
seventh

Sealy is 10th.
He is **last**.

Guided Learning

Look at the picture.
Answer the questions.

Greg

Kyle

Jason

1. How many children are climbing the wall?

2. Who is 1st?

3. Who is 2nd?

4. Who is 6th?

5 Who is 4th?

6 In which position is Ally?

7 In which position is Zack?

8 Who is last?

Let's Practice

Look at the picture.
Answer the questions.

1. Is anyone at home on the 1st floor?

2. On which floor is the cat?

3. On which floor is the dog sleeping?

4. On which floor is a man washing his hair?

5. On which floor is the goldfish?

6. What is on the 10th floor?

7. What is the man on the ninth floor doing?

ON YOUR OWN

Go to Workbook A:
Practice 1, pages 143–146

LESSON 2 Position Words

Lesson Objective

- Use position words to name relative positions.

Learn You can use position words to tell order and position.

Alan is **before** Ben.
Chris is **after** Ben.
Ben is **between** Alan and Chris.

Guided Learning

Name the positions of Demi and Evan using these words.

1. before   after   between

LEFT

RIGHT

The T-shirt is first on the **left**.
The pants are second from the left.

The T-shirt is fifth from the **right**.
It is also last from the right.

The towel is third from the left.
It is also third from the right.

The dress is **next to** the towel.
The dress is also next to the skirt.

The pants are between the T-shirt and the towel.

Guided Learning

Answer the questions.

Raj Megan Lin Dylan Mr. Smith Jorge

LEFT   RIGHT

2 Who is first on the right?

3 Who is second from the left?

4 Who is last from the left?

5 Who is next to Mr. Smith?

Who is between Dylan and Jorge?

Hands-On Activity

Carry out these activities.

1 Your teacher will choose ten children.
They should stand in a row facing the class.

Your teacher will ask the rest of you where each person is in the row.

Then take turns talking to your partner.
Talk about where each person is in the row.
Use these words:

1st	2nd	3rd	4th	5th	6th	7th	8th	9th	10th
	left		right		last		next to		

2 Put some school supplies in a row on your table.
Take turns with your partner.
Talk about where each thing is in the row.

Game

Find it First!

Players: 3
You need:
- 10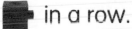
- 10

How to play: Use only 1, 2, or 3 fingers to count.

STEP 1 Players 1 and 2 put their 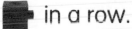 in a row.

STEP 2 Player 3 calls out an ordinal position.

9th from the left!

STEP 3 The first player to grab the correct 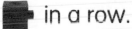 from his or her own row scores 1 point.

STEP 4 Put the 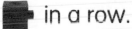 back. Player 3 then calls out another ordinal position. The first player to score 5 points wins.

STEP 5 Take turns calling out and playing.

Look at the picture.
Complete the sentences.

1. The black mouse is before the brown mouse.
   The white mouse is ⬚ the brown mouse.

2. The brown mouse is ⬚ the black mouse and the white mouse.

3. The peanut butter is second from the ⬚.

4. The cheese is ⬚ on the right.

5. The apple is ⬚ the peanut butter.

6. The potato is third from the ⬚ and the ⬚.

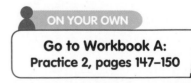

ON YOUR OWN

Go to Workbook A:
Practice 2, pages 147–150

You can use the picture to learn more position words.

Jasmine is **under** the table.

Shenice is **above** Pedro.
Pedro is **below** Shenice.

Danny is **behind** the curtains.
Jacob is **in front of** the curtains.

Guided Learning

Look at the picture.
Find the missing position words.

| under | above | below | behind | in front of |

6 Tom is ⬚ Sue.

7 Sue is ⬚ Tom.

8 The toys are ⬚ the books.

9 The books are ⬚ the toys.

10 The ball is ⬚ the shelf.

You can use the picture to learn more position words.

Mark is going **up** on the see-saw.
Tim is going **down** on the see-saw.

Kay is **near** the soccer ball.
Adele is **far** from the soccer ball.

Guided Learning

Look at the picture.
Find the missing position words.

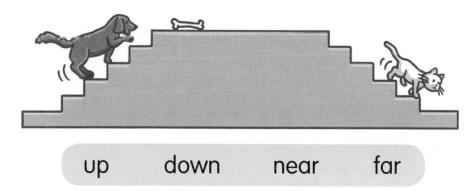

| up | down | near | far |

11 The dog is running ⬜ the stairs.

12 The dog is ⬜ the bone.

13 The cat is running ⬜ the stairs.

14 The cat is ⬜ from the bone.

Let's Practice

Short Sally

Quick Quentin

Tall Tom

Funny Fred

Tiny Tim

Look at the picture.
Answer the questions.

1 Who is below Short Sally?

2 Who is in front of Tapping Tina?

3 Who is above Tall Tom?

4 Who is under Bashful Betty's hat?

Mini Monkey

Hairy Harry

Tapping Tina

Bashful Betty

Sleeping Sam

RIGHT

5 Who is behind Sleeping Sam?

6 Who is sliding down the pole?

7 Who is climbing up the ladder?

8 Who is near the ball?

ON YOUR OWN

Go to Workbook A:
Practice 3, pages 151–152

Let's Explore!

Use nine  and one.

STEP 1 Mix the.
Then arrange the in a row.

STEP 2 Write the answer to each of these questions.
What is the position of the from the left?
What is the position of the from the right?

Position of from the Left	Position of from the Right	+

Repeat **STEP 1** and **STEP 2** to complete the chart.

The total number of is 10.

The answer in the is always more than the total number of.

Math Journal

Look around your classroom. Complete the sentences.

1. The books on the shelf are near the [ ].

2. My backpack is [ ] my table.

3. [ ] sits behind me.

4. The [ ] is far from me.

5. [ ] sits to the left of me.

CRITICAL THINKING SKILLS

Put On Your Thinking Cap!

PROBLEM SOLVING

Write the names in the correct order.

1. Annie Ant, Billy Beetle and Lizzy Lizard are in a line.
   Annie Ant is last.
   Billy Beetle is not 2nd.

   [ ]   [ ]   [ ]

   first

   Who is between 1st and 3rd?
   How do you know?

2 Tanya plants 4 flowers in a row.
The orchid is not 2nd from the left.
The daisy is between the rose and the sunflower.
The sunflower is 1st on the right.

LEFT   RIGHT

Which flower is 3rd from the right?
How do you know?

3 Joshua counts the number of children in his group.
Nick is the 4th person from the right.
He is also the 2nd person from the left.
How many people are there in his group?

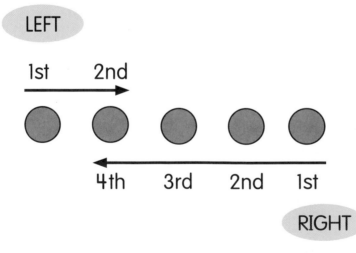

Draw a picture like this.

There are ⬚ children in the group.

4 Beth arranges 10 beads in a row.
There is only one red bead.
The red bead is placed 6th from the right.
If Beth counts from the left, in what position
is the red bead?

Draw a picture or **act it out**.

ON YOUR OWN

Go to Workbook A:
Put on Your Thinking Cap!
pages 153–156

Chapter Wrap Up

You have learned...

Ordinal Numbers and Position

Use ordinal and position words to talk about where things are

Hippo
3rd
third

Tury
6th
sixth

Billy
8th
eighth

Flipper
1st
first

Alice
5th
fifth

Wally
2nd
second

Ben
4th
fourth

Tyra
7th
seventh

Wally is after Flipper.
Wally is before Hippo.
Wally is between Flipper and Hippo.
Sealy is last.

The is first on the left.

The is first on the right.

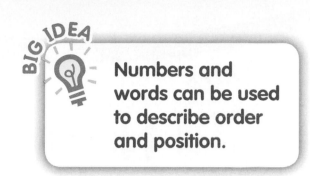

Numbers and words can be used to describe order and position.

Oscar
9th
ninth

Sealy
10th
tenth

Yellow is above blue.
Blue is below yellow.

Orange is in front of blue.
Blue is behind orange.

Pink is next to blue.

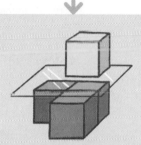

Brown is under the hand.

Orange is near yellow.
Blue is far from yellow.

Walk up the stairs.

Walk down the stairs.

ON YOUR OWN

**Go to Workbook A:
Chapter Review/Test,
pages 157–160**

Chapter 6 Ordinal Numbers and Position **167**

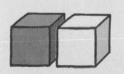

Recall Prior Knowledge

Counting

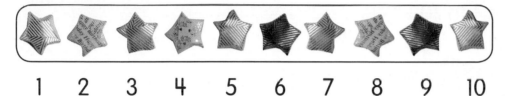

1 2 3 4 5 6 7 8 9 10

one, two, three... ten

Comparing

6 cubes

9 cubes

3 more

9 is greater than 6.
6 is less than 9.

Making patterns

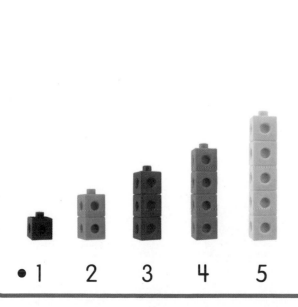

•1 2 3 4 5

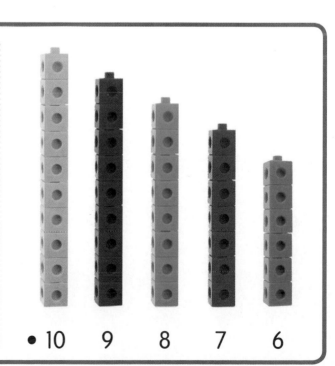

•10 9 8 7 6

Count.

1 Count from 1 to 10.

2 How many  are there?
Write the number and word. ⬜ ⬜

Find the missing numbers.

3

⬜ is greater than ⬜.

⬜ is less than ⬜.

Complete the number patterns.

4 6 7 8 ? ?

5 4 3 2 ? ?

1 Counting to 20

Lesson Objectives

- Count on from 10 to 20.
- Read and write 11 to 20 in numbers and words.

Vocabulary

eleven	twelve
thirteen	fourteen
fifteen	sixteen
seventeen	eighteen
nineteen	twenty

Learn **You can count on from 10.**

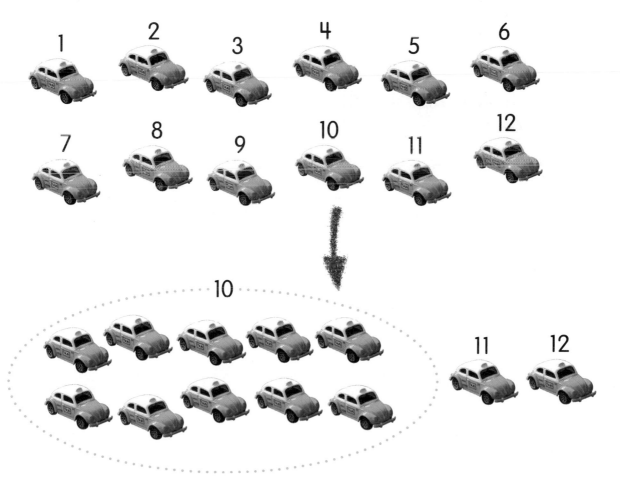

It is easier to count on: **10, 11, 12.**

You can count on from 10 using numbers and words.

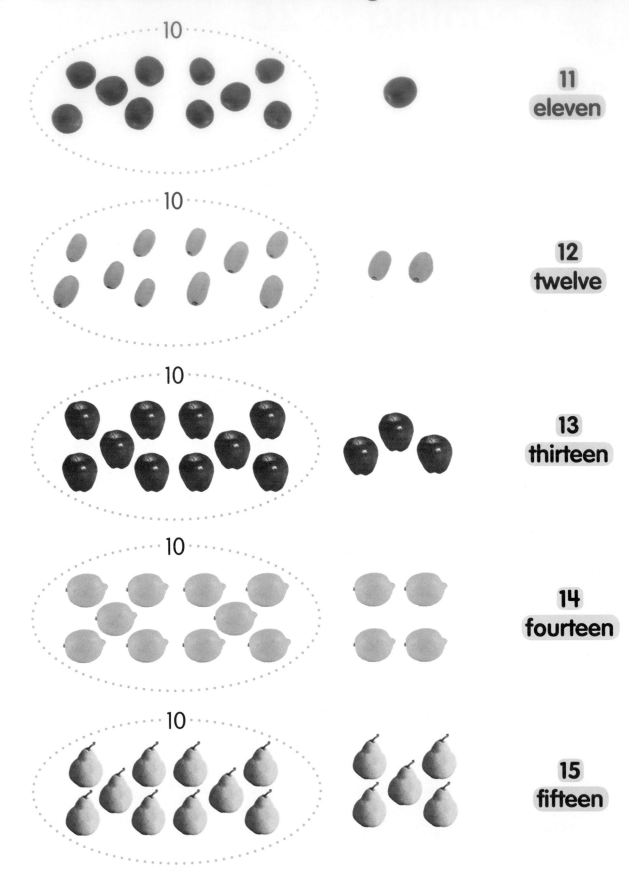

10   **11** eleven

10   **12** twelve

10   **13** thirteen

10   **14** fourteen

10   **15** fifteen

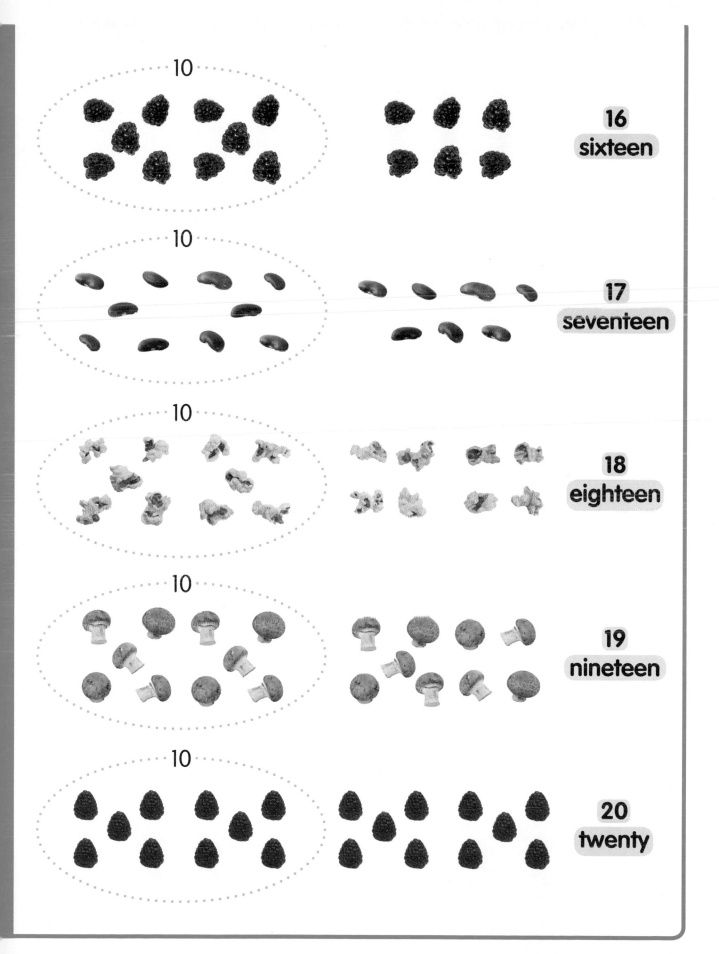

10   16 sixteen

10   17 seventeen

10   18 eighteen

10   19 nineteen

10   20 twenty

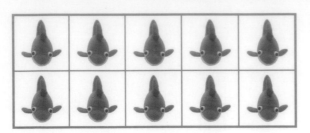

Learn — You can first make a ten. Then count on.

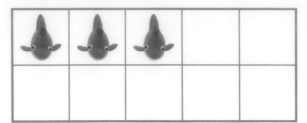

10 and 3 make 13.
Ten and three make thirteen.
10 + 3 = 13

Guided Learning

Make a ten.
Then count on.

1

Ten and four make _____.
_____ and _____ make 14.

_____ + _____ = _____

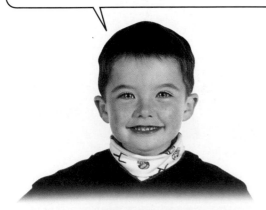

WORKING TOGETHER Game

Roll the Number Cube!

Players: 4
You need:
- one number cube
- base ten blocks

STEP 1 Roll the number cube.
Then take this number of .

6!

STEP 2 Each player take turns to roll the number cube and take .

STEP 3 On your next turn, roll the number cube again.
Then take this number of .
If you have 10 , trade them for one ▬▬▬▬.

6 + 4 = 10!

The first player to get 2 ▬▬▬▬ wins!

Guided Learning

Find the missing numbers.

2 10 and 7 make ▢ .   10 + 7 = ▢

3 10 and 10 make ▢ .   10 + 10 = ▢

Let's Practice

Make a ten.
Then count on.

1

10 and 3 make ▢ .   10 + 3 = ▢

2

10 and ▢ make ▢ .   10 + ▢ = ▢

ON YOUR OWN

Go to Workbook A:
Practice 1, pages 167–172

2 Place Value

Lesson Objectives

- Use a place-value chart to show numbers up to 20.
- Show objects up to 20 as tens and ones.

Vocabulary
place-value chart

Learn **You can use place value to show numbers to 20.**

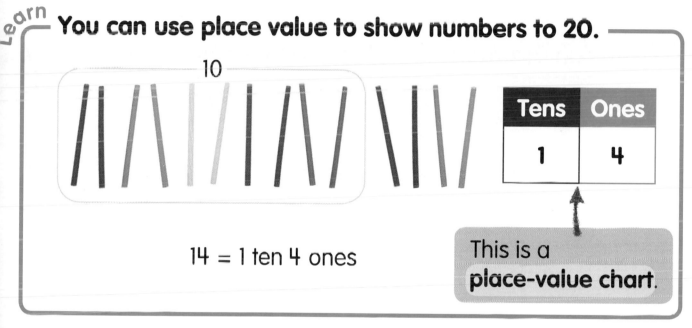

14 = 1 ten 4 ones

This is a **place-value chart**.

Guided Learning

Use place value to find the missing numbers.

1

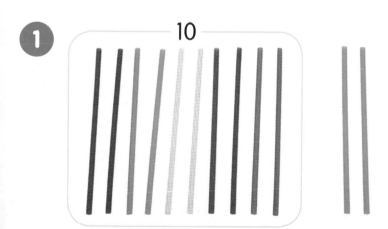

12 = ⬭ ten ⬭ ones

2

10

Tens	Ones

16 = ⬭ ten ⬭ ones

 Learn You can use models to show numbers to 20.

13 = 1 ten 3 ones

Tens	Ones
1	**3**
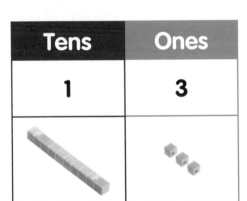	

Guided Learning

Find the correct place-value chart for the number.

3 15

Tens	Ones

Tens	Ones

Tens	Ones

4 17

Tens	Ones		Tens	Ones		Tens	Ones

Hands-On Activity

Use and a place-value chart.

STEP 1 Group the to show these numbers.

a 18 **b** 20

STEP 2 Draw ▯ for tens and □ for ones in the place-value chart.

Example

15

Tens	Ones
1	5
▯	□ □ □ □ □

Let's Practice

Look at each place-value chart.
What is the number shown?

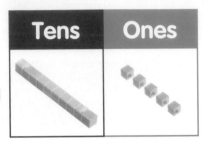

1

Tens	Ones

2

Tens	Ones

Show the number.
Draw ▯ for tens and □ for ones.

3

14

Tens	Ones

4

17

Tens	Ones

Find the missing numbers.

5 11 = ⬤ ten ⬤ one

6 10 = ⬤ ten ⬤ ones

7 16 = ⬤ ten ⬤ ones

8 18 = ⬤ ten ⬤ ones

ON YOUR OWN

Go to Workbook A:
Practice 2, pages 173–176

Comparing Numbers

Lesson Objective

- Compare numbers to 20.

Vocabulary
greatest
least

Compare sets and numbers.

Set A

12

Set B

10

Set A has 2 more than Set B.

Set B has 2 fewer than Set A.

12 is greater than 10.

10 is less than 12.

Guided Learning

Count.
Then answer the questions.

1 Set A

⬜

Set B

⬜

2 Which set has more? ⬜

3 How many more? ⬜

4 Which set has fewer? ⬜

5 How many fewer? ⬜

6 ⬜ is greater than ⬜.

7 ⬜ is less than ⬜.

You can use place value to find how much greater or how much less.

Compare 13 and 15.
Which number is greater?
How much greater is the number?

13

15

Tens	Ones
1	3

Tens	Ones
1	5

First, compare the tens.
The tens are equal.
Then, compare the ones.

The ones are not equal.
5 is greater than 3 by 2.
So, 15 is greater than 13 by 2.

Guided Learning

Compare the numbers.
Use place value to help you.

8 Which number is greater?
How much greater?

Tens	Ones
1	9

19

Tens	Ones
1	7

17

[____] is greater than [____].

[____] is greater than [____] by [____].

9 Which number is less?
How much less?

Tens	Ones
1	6

16

Tens	Ones
1	2

12

[____] is less than [____].

[____] is less than [____] by [____].

You can use place value to compare three numbers.

Compare 14, 11 and 16.

Tens	Ones
1	4

Tens	Ones
1	1

Tens	Ones
1	6

The tens are all equal.
So, compare the ones.

4 is greater than 1.
6 is greater than 4.

16 is the **greatest** number.
11 is the **least** number.

Guided Learning

Compare the numbers.
Use place value to help you.

10 Which is the greatest?
     Which is the least?

   10   17   12

   _____ is the greatest number.

   _____ is the least number.

Tens	Ones

Count and compare.

1 Which set has more?

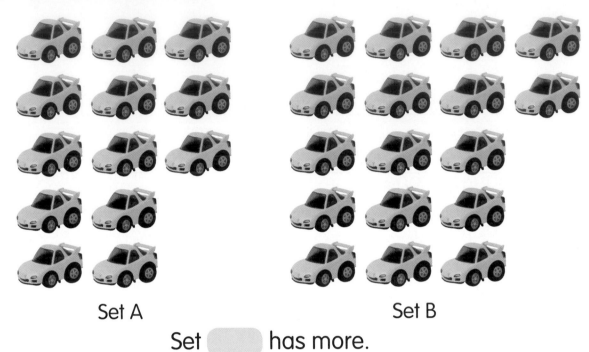

Set A   Set B

Set [   ] has more.

2 Which set has fewer?

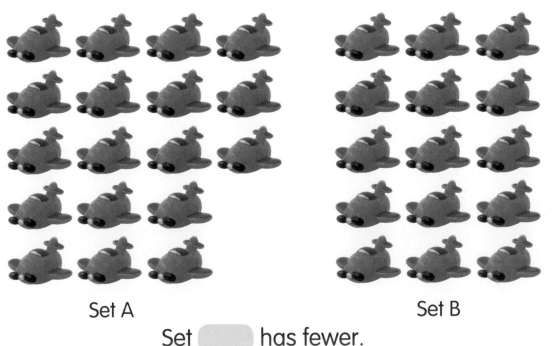

Set A   Set B

Set [   ] has fewer.

Which number is greater?
How much greater?

3 (9) or (5)

( ) is greater.

It is greater by ( ).

Which number is less?
How much less?

4 (19) or (10)

( ) is less.

It is less by ( ).

Compare these numbers.

5 [12] (18) ☆ 14

Which is the least? ( )

Which is the greatest? ( )

6 ◇ 11 ⬠ 20 ✶ 10

Which is the least? ( )

Which is the greatest? ( )

ON YOUR OWN

Go to Workbook A:
Practice 3, pages 177–184

Let's Explore!

Use .
Look at these numbers.

11   15   12

STEP 1 Make a number train for the greatest number.
Name it Train G.

STEP 2 Make a number train for the least number.
Name it Train L.

STEP 3 Take some 🔲 from Train G to give to Train L.
Make both trains have the same number of 🔲.

How many 🔲 must you take from Train G?

Example
Greatest number = 15

Train G

Least number = 11

Train L

Take 2 🔲 from Train G.
Put them on Train L.

Repeat **STEP 1** to **STEP 3** for these numbers.

ⓐ 16   11   19

ⓑ 20   12   17

LESSON 4 Making Patterns and Ordering Numbers

Lesson Objective

• Order numbers by making number patterns.

Vocabulary
order

Learn · You can make a pattern.

Lisa uses to make a pattern.

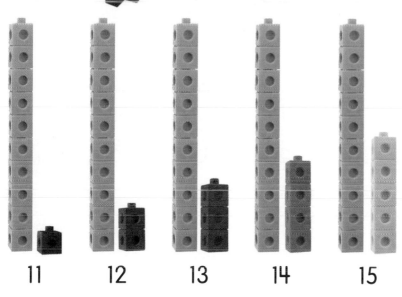

| 11 | 12 | 13 | 14 | 15 | ? |

How many come next in the pattern?

$$+1 \quad +1 \quad +1 \quad +1 \quad +1$$
11, 12, 13, 14, 15, 16

Each number is 1 more than the number before it.

16 comes next in the pattern.

Guided Learning

Complete the patterns.

1 Jenny uses beads to make a pattern.

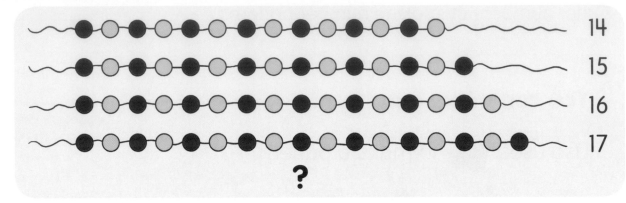

14

15

16

17

?

How many beads come next in the pattern? [____]

2 10, 11, 12, 13, [____], [____], [____]

13, 14, 15, 16!

3 14, 15, 16, 17, [____], [____], [____]

4 20, 19, 18, 17, [____], [____], [____]

Learn

You can find a number more than another number.

What is 1 more than 15?

↓ 1 more

1 more than 15 is 16.

Guided Learning

Solve.

5 What is 2 more than 17?

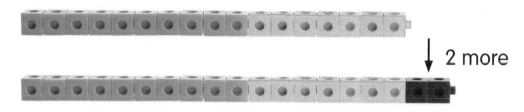

2 more

2 more than 17 is _____ .

Learn **You can find a number less than another number.**

What is 1 less than 16?

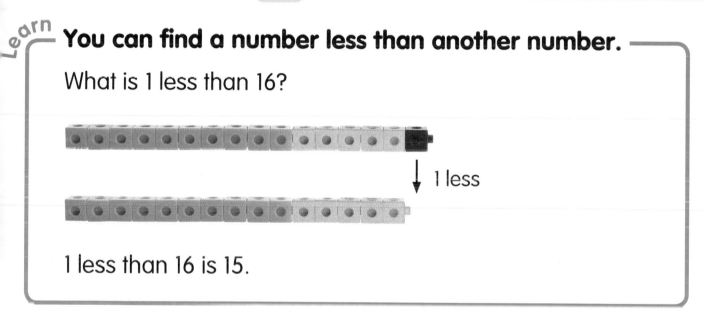

1 less

1 less than 16 is 15.

Guided Learning

Solve.

6 What is 2 less than 20?

2 less

2 less than 20 is _____ .

You can **order** numbers from least to greatest.

Compare these numbers.

(14) (18) (12)

The tens are all equal.
So, compare the ones.

4 is greater than 2.
8 is greater than 4.

18 is the greatest number.
12 is the least number.

Ordered from least to greatest,
the numbers are:

(12)   (14)   (18)

least   greatest

Guided Learning

Order the numbers.

7 from greatest to least

(20)   (2)   (13)

8 from least to greatest

(8)   (10)   (18)

Let's Practice

Find the missing numbers.

1 2 more than 13 is ⬭ .

2 3 less than 19 is ⬭ .

Find the missing numbers.
Use the picture to help you.

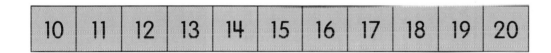

| 10 | 11 | 12 | 13 | 14 | 15 | 16 | 17 | 18 | 19 | 20 |

3 2 more than 12 is ⬭ .

4 2 more than 18 is ⬭ .

5 3 more than 10 is ⬭ .

6 ⬭ is 2 less than 18.

7 ⬭ is 2 less than 17.

8 ⬭ is 3 less than 20.

Complete the patterns.

9 11, 12, 13, _____, 15, 16

10 17, 16, 15, _____, _____, 12, 11

11 7, 9, _____, 13, 15, _____, 19

12 _____, 18, 16, _____, _____, 10, 8

Order the numbers from greatest to least.

13 11   9   18   15

Order the numbers from least to greatest.

14 20   6   12   16

ON YOUR OWN

Go to Workbook A:
Practice 4, pages 185–188

PROBLEM SOLVING

Find the two missing numbers in the pattern. Then put the cards in order.

 1　　| 10 | 14 | 16 | 20 |　　| ? | ? |

2　　| 12 | 14 | 15 | 16 |　　| ? | ? |

There is more than one correct answer for Question 2.

ON YOUR OWN

**Go to Workbook A:
Put on Your Thinking Cap!
pages 189–192**

Chapter Wrap Up

You have learned...

Numbers to 20

Count

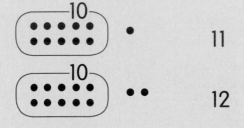

10 • 11

10 •• 12

10 ••• 13

10 •••• 14

10 ••••• 15

10 ••••• • 16

10 ••••• •• 17

10 ••••• ••• 18

10 ••••• •••• 19

10 ••••• ••••• 20

Read and Write

11	eleven
12	twelve
13	thirteen
14	fourteen
15	fifteen
16	sixteen
17	seventeen
18	eighteen
19	nineteen
20	twenty

Use a Place-Value Chart

Tens	Ones
1	4

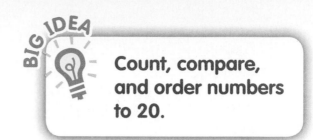

Count, compare, and order numbers to 20.

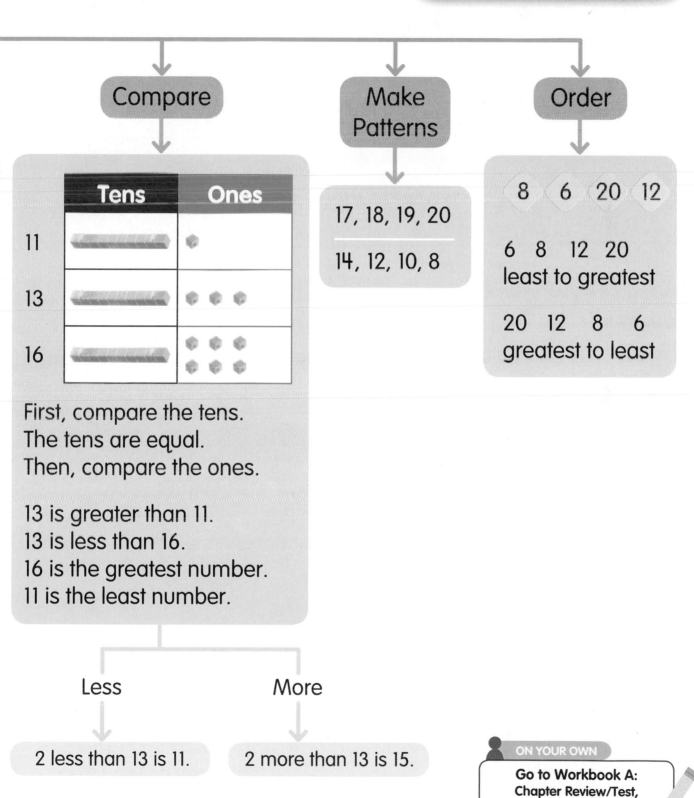

Compare

Tens	Ones
11	
13	
16	

First, compare the tens.
The tens are equal.
Then, compare the ones.

13 is greater than 11.
13 is less than 16.
16 is the greatest number.
11 is the least number.

Less

2 less than 13 is 11.

More

2 more than 13 is 15.

Make Patterns

17, 18, 19, 20

14, 12, 10, 8

Order

8 6 20 12

6 8 12 20
least to greatest

20 12 8 6
greatest to least

ON YOUR OWN

**Go to Workbook A:
Chapter Review/Test,
pages 193–196**

Addition and Subtraction Facts to 20

BIG IDEA

Different strategies can be used to add and subtract.

Recall Prior Knowledge

Using fact families to solve number sentences

$1 + 3 = 4$
$3 + 1 = 4$
$4 - 1 = 3$
$4 - 3 = 1$

$? - 1 = 3$

$1 + 3 = 4$ is the related addition fact.
So, $4 - 1 = 3$.

$3 + ? = 4$

$4 - 3 = 1$ is the related subtraction fact.
So, $3 + 1 = 4$.

Adding and subtracting 0

$3 + 0 = 3$
$3 - 0 = 3$

Addition facts

10 and 2 make 12.
12 is 10 and 2.
$10 + 2 = 12$

Comparing numbers

15 is 2 more than 13.

14 is 3 less than 17.

Make a fact family.

1   4   7   3

$$\boxed{} + \boxed{} = \boxed{}$$
$$\boxed{} + \boxed{} = \boxed{}$$
$$\boxed{} - \boxed{} = \boxed{}$$
$$\boxed{} - \boxed{} = \boxed{}$$

Complete the number sentences.
Use related facts.

2 $\boxed{} + 4 = 7$

   $7 - \boxed{} = 3$

Solve.

3 $9 + 1 = 10$

   $1 + \boxed{} = 10$

4 $5 + 0 = \boxed{}$

5 $5 - \boxed{} = 5$

6   10 and 4 make $\boxed{}$.

   14 is $\boxed{}$ and 4.

   $10 + \boxed{} = 14$

7 $\boxed{}$ is 3 more than 15.

8   5 less than 20 is $\boxed{}$.

LESSON 1 Ways to Add

Lesson Objective

- Use different strategies to add 1- and 2-digit numbers.

Vocabulary

group	doubles fact
same	doubles plus one

You can add by making a 10.

Gus has 8 cherries.
Ava gives him 6 more.

How many cherries does Gus have now?

Step 1 Make a **group** of 10 cherries.

8   +   6

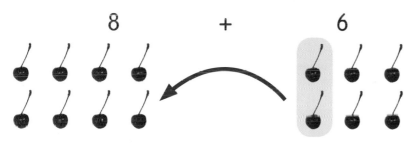

You can break the number that is less into 2 parts.

$8 + 6 = 10 + 4$
$ = 14$

Step 2 Add the cherries that are left over to the group of 10.

10   +   4

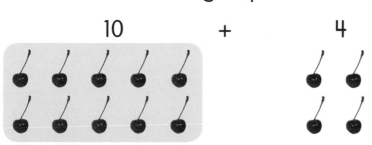

$10 + 4 = 14$
Gus has 14 cherries now.

 Hands-On Activity

Use .

Group the 🔴⚪ to make a 10.
Then add.

Example

9   +   3

⚪⚪⚪⚪⚪⚪⚪⚪⚪   🔴🔴🔴

10   +   2

⚪⚪⚪⚪⚪⚪⚪⚪⚪🔴   🔴🔴

> $9 + 3 = 10 + 2$
> $= 12$

1   8   +   6

⚪⚪⚪⚪⚪⚪⚪⚪🔴🔴   🔴🔴🔴🔴

> $8 + 6 = 10 + \boxed{}$
> $= \boxed{}$

2   7   +   6

⚪⚪⚪⚪   🔴🔴🔴
⚪⚪⚪   🔴🔴🔴

> $7 + 6 = 10 + \boxed{}$
> $= \boxed{}$

Guided Learning

Make a 10.
Then add.
Use number bonds to help you.

1 9 + 5 =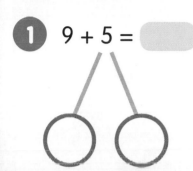

2 8 + 7 =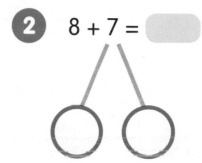

Let's Practice

Make a 10.
Then add.

1 9 + 4 =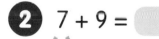

2 7 + 9 =

3 9 + 8 =

4 8 + 3 = 10 +

=

5 6 + 8 = 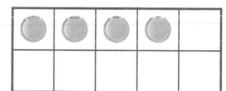 +

=

ON YOUR OWN

Go to Workbook A:
Practice 1, pages 197–202

Learn

You can add by grouping into a 10 and ones.

Paul has 16 dinosaurs.
His sister gives him 3 more dinosaurs.
How many dinosaurs does Paul have now?

Step 1 Group 16 into a 10 and ones.
16 = 10 + 6

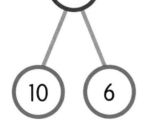

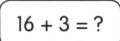

16 + 3 = ?

Step 2 Add the ones.
6 + 3 = 9

Step 3 Add the 10 and ones.
10 + 9 = 19

So, 16 + 3 = 19.

Paul has 19 dinosaurs now.

204   **Chapter 8** Addition and Subtraction Facts to 20

Guided Learning

**Group into a 10 and ones.
Then add.**

3 $13 + 3 = \boxed{}$

4 $12 + 7 = \boxed{}$

Let's Practice

**Group into a 10 and ones.
Then add.**

1 $11 + 7 = \boxed{}$

2 $4 + 13 = \boxed{}$

3 $14 + 5 = \boxed{}$

4 $2 + 17 = \boxed{}$

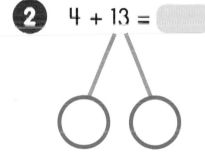

ON YOUR OWN

Go to Workbook A:
Practice 2, pages 203–204

This is a **doubles fact**.

$$2 + 2 = 4$$

Double 2 means to add 2 more to 2.
The numbers that are added are the **same**.

Here are more doubles facts.

$$3 + 3 = 6$$

$$4 + 4 = 8$$

Guided Learning

Solve.

5 Which is the doubles fact?
$1 + 1 = 2$ or $10 + 1 = 11$

                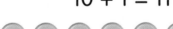

6 Double 5 means add [   ] more to 5.

7 $5 + 5 =$ [   ]

You can use doubles plus one facts to add.

2 + 2 = 4 is a doubles fact.

What is 2 + 3?

2 + 3 = ?

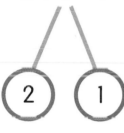

You can rewrite 2 + 3 like this:
    2 + 2 + 1
So, 2 + 3 is double 2 plus 1.

2 + 3 is a **doubles plus one** fact.
You can use the doubles fact 2 + 2 to add 2 and 3.

$\underline{2 + 2} = 4$ $2 + 3 = \underline{2 + 2 + 1}$
doubles   doubles plus 1
                                          = 4 + 1
                                          = 5

2 + 2 and 1 more.

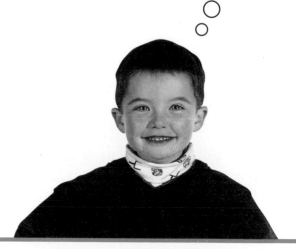

Guided Learning

Solve.

8 Which are the doubles facts?
Which are the doubles plus one facts?

$4 + 4 = 8$ $\qquad$ $4 + 5 = 9$ $\qquad$ $8 + 7 = 15$ $\qquad$ $7 + 7 = 14$

9 $5 + 6 = ?$

5 + 6 is double ⬭ plus ⬭ .

5 + 6 = 5 + ⬭ + ⬭

$\qquad$ = 10 + ⬭

$\qquad$ = ⬭

Let's Practice

Solve.

1 **ⓐ** Double 6 is ⬭ + ⬭ = ⬭

ⓑ 6 + 7 = ⬭ + ⬭ + ⬭

$\qquad$ = ⬭

2 **ⓐ** What doubles fact helps you to add 9 and 8? ⬭

ⓑ 9 + 8 = ⬭

ON YOUR OWN

Go to Workbook A:
Practice 3, pages 205–208

LESSON 2 Ways to Subtract

Lesson Objective

• Subtract a 1-digit from a 2-digit number with and without grouping.

Learn

You can subtract by grouping into a 10 and ones.

Ray has 17 toy cars.
He gives away 3 toy cars.
How many cars does he have left?

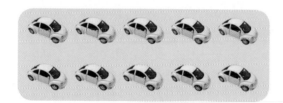

Step 1 Group 17 into a 10 and ones.
$17 = 10 + 7$

$$17 - 3 = ?$$

17
/ \
10   7

$17 - 3 = ?$

Step 2 Subtract the ones.
$7 - 3 = 4$

Step 3 Add the 10 and the ones.
$10 + 4 = 14$

So, $17 - 3 = 14$.

Ray has 14 toy cars left.

Guided Learning

**Group the numbers into a 10 and ones.
Then subtract.**

1 17 – 5 = ⬚

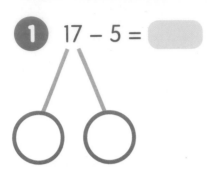

2 18 – 3 = ⬚

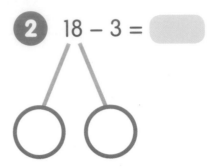

**Solve the riddle.
Subtract, then write the letter on the correct line.**

3 13 – 3 = ◯ **T**   17 – 6 = ◯ **S**

15 – 3 = ◯ **H**   18 – 5 = ◯ **W**

16 – 1 = ◯ **E**   19 – 3 = ◯ **I**

17 – 0 = ◯ **U**   18 – 4 = ◯ **O**

Where does the President of the United States live?

THE

___ ___ ___ ___ ___
13   12   16   10   15

___ ___ ___ ___ ___
12   14   17   11   15

You can subtract by grouping into a 10 and ones.

Shawn makes 12 stars.
He gives 7 to Gina.
How many stars does Shawn have left?

Step 1 Group 12 into a 10 and ones.
12 = 10 + 2

(12) − 7 = ?

2   10

Step 2 You cannot take away 7 from 2.
So, subtract 7 from 10.
10 − 7 = 3

Step 3 Add the ones.
2 + 3 = 5

So, 12 − 7 = 5.

Shawn has 5 stars left.

Guided Learning

**Group the numbers into a 10 and ones.
Then subtract.**

4 $11 - 3 =$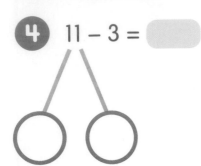

5 $13 - 6 =$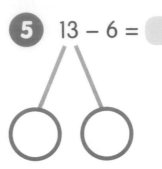

Learn **You can use doubles facts of addition to help you subtract.**

Joe buys 12 eggs.
He uses 6 eggs to bake a cake.

$6 + 6 = 12$
So, $12 - 6 = 6$

$12 - 6 = 6$
Joe has 6 eggs left.

Guided Learning

Solve.

6 $10 - 5 =$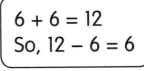

7 $14 - 7 =$

 **Game**

Spin and Subtract!

Players: 3

You need:
- 2 spinners (A and B)

How to play:

 Spinner A

 Spinner B

STEP 1 Player 1 uses Spinner A to get a number.

STEP 2 Player 1 then uses Spinner B to get a another number.

STEP 3 Player 2 and Player 3 subtract the two numbers.

STEP 4 The player who gets the right subtraction sentence first gets 1 point. Take turns spinning the spinner.

The player who gets the most points after six rounds wins!

Let's Practice

Subtract.
You can use number bonds to help you.

1 16 − 3 = [ ]

2 17 − 4 = [ ]

3 18 − 7 = [ ]

4 19 − 5 = [ ]

5 15 − 6 = [ ]

6 12 − 5 = [ ]

7 11 − 4 = [ ]

8 14 − 8 = [ ]

9 20 − 9 = [ ]

10 18 − 9 = [ ]

ON YOUR OWN

Go to Workbook A:
Practice 4, pages 209–216

Real-World Problems: Addition and Subtraction Facts

Lesson Objective

• Solve real-world problems.

Learn **Add to solve this word problem.**

Ramon has 9 .

Ana gives him 6 .

How many does Ramon have in all?

$$9 + 6 = 15$$

Ramon has 15 in all.

Guided Learning

Solve.

1 Lin makes 6 pasta rings.
Kate makes 6 pasta rings.
How many pasta rings do they
make in all?

◯◯◯ = ◯

They make ◯ pasta rings in all.

Subtract to solve this word problem.

Ali has 16 clay shells.
He gives Mani 5 clay shells.
How many clay shells does Ali have left?

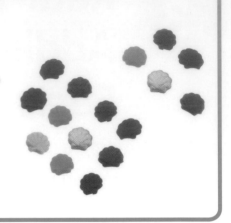

$$16 - 5 = 11$$

Ali has 11 clay shells left.

Guided Learning

Solve.

2 George has 11 paper clips.
3 paper clips are blue.
The rest are red.
How many paper clips are red?

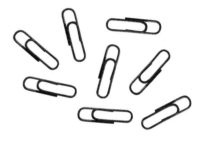

 =

 paper clips are red.

Let's Practice

Solve.

1 Terry picks 8 tomatoes.
Nan picks 8 tomatoes.
How many tomatoes do Terry
and Nan have in all?

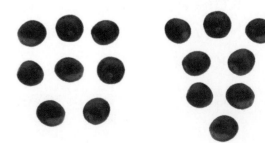

 =

They have tomatoes in all.

2 Pam makes 14 paper flowers.
9 are blue.
How many are pink?

[____] [__] [____] = [____]

[____] flowers are pink.

3 Walter finds 15 leaves.
His brother gives him 4 more leaves.
How many leaves does Walter have in all?

[____] [__] [____] = [____]

Walter has [____] leaves in all.

4 Junie gives away 8 oranges.
She has 9 oranges left.
How many oranges did she have at first?

What is the doubles fact?

⬜ ⬤ ⬜ = ⬜

Junie had ⬜ oranges at first.

5 Tim has 16 marbles.
He loses some and has 8 marbles left.
How many marbles does he lose?

⬜ ⬤ ⬜ = ⬜

Tim loses ⬜ marbles.

ON YOUR OWN

Go to Workbook A:
Practice 5, pages 217–218

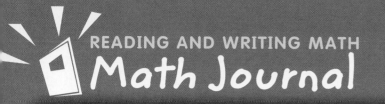

READING AND WRITING MATH
Math Journal

Look at the people around you.
Write an addition or subtraction story about them.
Use a number bond to help you.

Example

There are 12 children in my class.
3 children have blonde hair.
The rest have brown hair.
How many children have brown hair?

⬤12 – 3 = ▢

⬤2   ⬤10

▢ children have brown hair.

Let's Explore!

Make number sentences using these numbers.
You can use each number more than once.

(5) (6) (7) (8) (9) (13) (15)

How many fact families can you make? [____]

CRITICAL THINKING SKILLS
Put On Your Thinking Cap!

PROBLEM SOLVING

1 Fill in the ● and ● with these numbers.

(3) (4) (5) (6) (7) (15)

➡ and ⬇ mean =.
Use each number once.

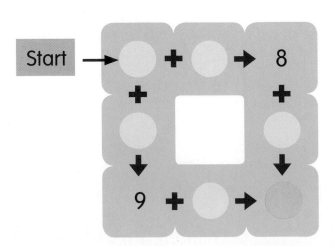

The number in the ● is the greatest.

PROBLEM SOLVING

2 Fill in the ◯ and ◯ with these numbers.

(3) (4) (6) (7) (8) (17)

→ and ↓ mean =.
Use each number once.

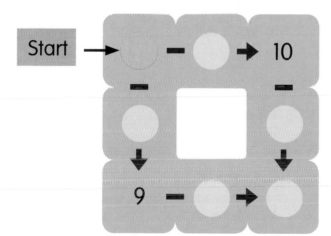

Chapter Wrap Up
You have learned...

Addition and Subtraction Facts to 20

to add by making a 10.

$$8 + 5 = 10 + 3$$
$$= 13$$

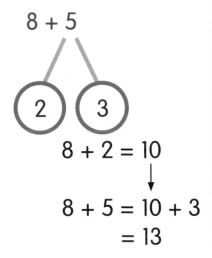

$8 + 5$

$8 + 2 = 10$

$$8 + 5 = 10 + 3$$
$$= 13$$

to add by grouping into a 10 and ones.

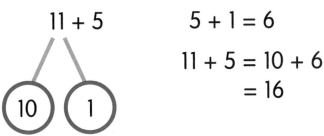

$11 + 5$

$5 + 1 = 6$

$$11 + 5 = 10 + 6$$
$$= 16$$

to add using doubles facts.

$3 + 3 = 6$ is a doubles fact.
The numbers that are added are the same.

to add using doubles plus one.

$3 + 4$ is $3 + 3$ plus 1
$$3 + 4 = 3 + 3 + 1$$
$$= 7$$

BIG IDEA Different strategies can be used to add and subtract.

to subtract by grouping into a 10 and ones.

1 15 − 3

10   5

5 − 3 = 2

15 − 3 = 10 + 2
= 12

2 15 − 6

5   10

10 − 6 = 4

15 − 6 = 4 + 5
= 9

to subtract using doubles facts.

7 + 7 = 14
So, 14 − 7 = 7.

to add or subtract to solve real-world problems.

1 Joy has 8 tadpoles.
Ben gives her 5 more tadpoles.
How many tadpoles does she have now?

8 + 5 = 13

Joy has 13 tadpoles now.

2 Con has 18 marbles.
He gives Pete 9 marbles.
How many marbles does Con have left?

18 − 9 = 9

Con has 9 marbles left.

ON YOUR OWN

Go to Workbook A:
Chapter Review/Test,
pages 223–224

CHAPTER
9 Length

BIG IDEA

Compare the height and length of things. Measure with non-standard units to find length.

Recall Prior Knowledge

Counting

There are 4 in all.

....

There are 4 in all.

....

There are 4 \ in all.

Comparing numbers

(8) (20) (10)

8 is the least number.
20 is the greatest number.

Count.
How many are there?

1

There are ⬭ ◗ in all.

2

There are ⬭ ▪ in all.

3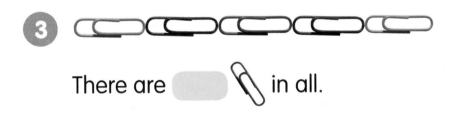

There are ⬭ ⌇ in all.

Compare these numbers.

4 | 18 | 8 | 12 |

Which is the greatest? ⬭

Which is the least? ⬭

LESSON 1 Comparing Two Things

Lesson Objective

- Compare two lengths using the terms tall/taller, long/longer, and short/shorter.

Vocabulary

tall	taller
short	shorter
long	longer

Learn You can compare the height of people.

I am **tall**.

I am **taller**.

I am **short**.

I am **shorter**.

Guided Learning

**Look at your desk and your teacher's desk.
Answer the questions.**

1 Which is taller?

2 Which is shorter?

You can compare the length of things.

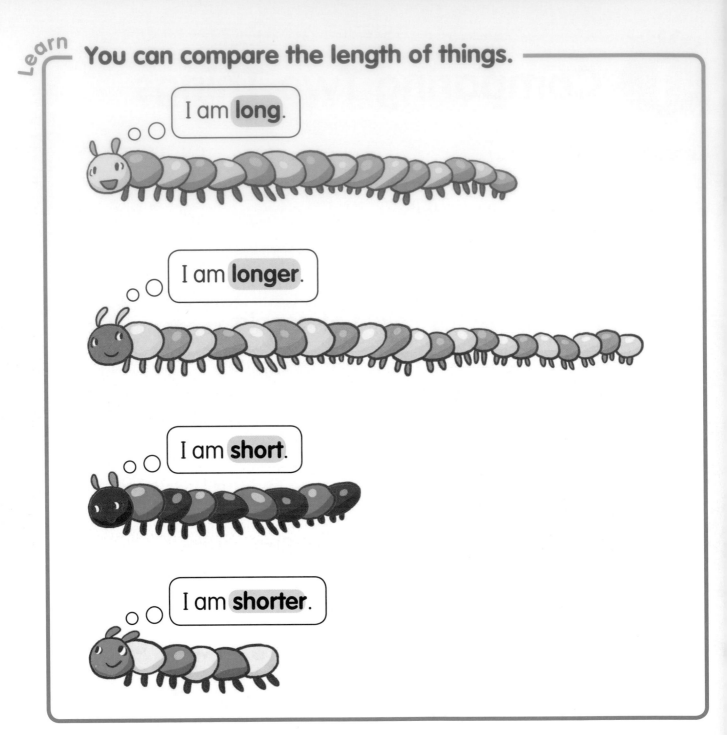

I am **long**.

I am **longer**.

I am **short**.

I am **shorter**.

Guided Learning

Look at your pencil and your friend's pencil.
Answer the questions.

3 Whose pencil is longer?

4 Whose pencil is shorter?

 Hands-On Activity

Use 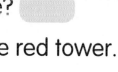.

1 **ⓐ** Make a tower with 3 ▪️.

ⓑ Make a tower taller than the red tower.
Use ◼️.
How many cubes did you use? ⬜

Red Tower

ⓒ Make a tower shorter than the red tower.
Use ◼️.
How many cubes did you use? ⬜

2 **ⓐ** Make a number train with 5 ◼️.

Green Train

ⓑ Make a train longer than the green train.
Use ◻️.
How many cubes did you use? ⬜

ⓒ Make a train shorter than the green train.
Use ◼️.
How many cubes did you use? ⬜

Look around your classroom.

3 Find something shorter than your pencil. ⬜

Find something longer than your pencil. ⬜

WORK IN PAIRS

Papa Cat and Little Cat are sewing!
Talk about this picture with a friend.
Use these words.

tall   taller

long   longer

short   shorter

> Little Cat's tail is long.
> Papa Cat's tail is longer.

Let's Practice

Look at the pictures.
Solve.

ruler

pencil

1 Which is longer?

2 Which is shorter?

a The pencil is _____ than the ruler.

b The ruler is _____ than the pencil.

3 Who is shorter?

4 Who is taller?

Terry   Brian

ON YOUR OWN

Go to Workbook A:
Practice 1, pages 225–228

LESSON 2 Comparing More Than Two Things

Lesson Objectives

- Compare two lengths by comparing each with a third length.
- Compare more than two lengths using the terms tallest, longest, and shortest.

Learn **You can compare the height of more than two people.**

Chris   Brandon   Annie

Chris is taller than Brandon.
Brandon is taller than Annie.
So, Chris is taller than Annie.

Guided Learning

Fill in the blanks.

1

The red scarf is longer than the blue scarf.

The blue scarf is longer than the ⬚ scarf.

So, the red scarf is longer than the ⬚ scarf.

Learn You can compare the height and length of more than two people or things.

(Annie) (Brandon) (Chris)

Chris is the **tallest**.
Annie is the **shortest**.

Annie has the **longest** scarf.
Brandon has the **shortest** scarf.

Look at the picture.
Answer the questions.

Pablo and Erin see some animals in the zoo.

2 Which is the tallest animal?

3 Which is the shortest animal?

4 Which is the longest animal?

5 Which is the shortest animal?

Hands-On Activity

Use .

STEP 1 Make four towers like this. Then place them in order. You may start with the tallest or the shortest tower.

STEP 2 Make a tower taller than the tallest tower.

STEP 3 Make a tower shorter than the shortest tower.

Look around your classroom. Find these things.

1 the longest thing

2 the tallest thing

3 the shortest thing

Rearrange the letters to solve.

T E H   S T A U T E   F O   L I E B R T Y

Which is the longest word?

Let's Practice

Compare.
Answer the questions.

Lee Tania Will

1 Who is taller, Lee or Will?

2 Who is taller, Tania or Will?

3 Is Tania taller than Lee?

4 Who is the tallest?

5 Who is the shortest?

ON YOUR OWN

Go to Workbook A:
Practice 2, pages 229–233

LESSON 3 Using a Start Line

Lesson Objective

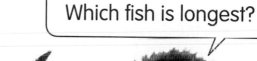

- Use a common starting point when comparing lengths.

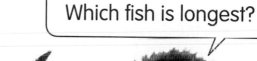 **Vocabulary**
start line

Learn **You can compare the length of things with a start line.**

Which fish is longest?

Now, can you tell which fish is the longest?

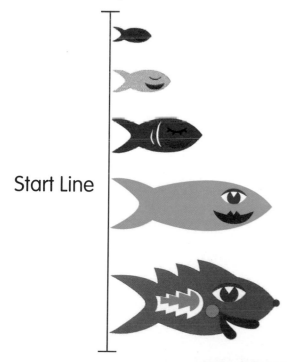

Start Line

The blue fish is longest.

Putting things at a **start line** helps you to see which is the longest.

Hands-On Activity

Use .

1 Cut out copies of these strips of paper.
Put them at a start line.

Which is longest? ⬚

Which is shortest? ⬚

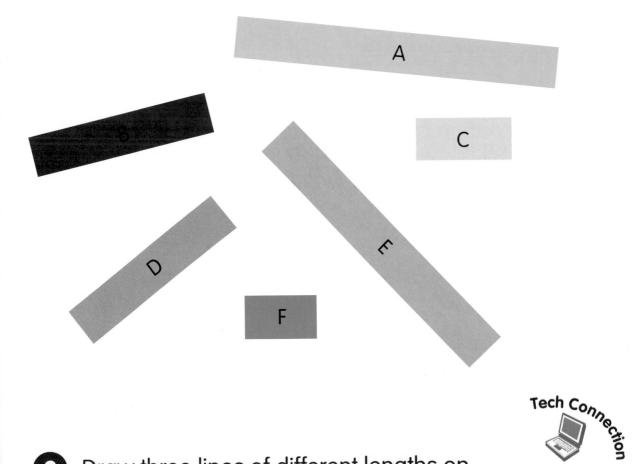

2 Draw three lines of different lengths on the computer.
Ask your friend which is longest and which is shortest.

Tech Connection

Let's Practice

Solve.

A

1 **ⓐ** Which ribbon is longer than Ribbon A?
Name it Ribbon B.

ⓑ Which ribbon is shorter than Ribbon A?
Name it Ribbon C.

ⓒ Which ribbon is the longest?
Which ribbon is the shortest?

2 **ⓐ** Which is the tallest building?

ⓑ Which is the shortest building?

ⓒ Which building is as tall as Building Q?

P   Q   R   S   T

ON YOUR OWN

Go to Workbook A:
Practice 3, pages 235–236

4 Measuring Things

Lesson Objectives

- Measure lengths using non-standard units.

- Understand that using different non-standard units may give different measurements for the same item.

Vocabulary
about

 Learn **You can measure length with objects.**

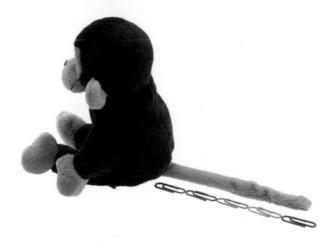

The monkey's tail is **about** 5 paper clips long.
You can also say that its length is about 5 paper clips.

Guided Learning

Complete.

1

The stapler is about [ ] paper clips long.

2

The bag is about [ ] spoons long.

✋ Hands-On Activity

Use / **to measure.**

the teacher's table [ ]

your desk [ ]

your textbook [ ]

Then answer the questions.

1 Which is the longest? [ ]

2 Which is the shortest? [ ]

3 Is your desk longer than the teacher's desk? [ ]

Learn You can use different objects to measure the same thing.

The pencil is about 5 paper clips long.
It is about 1 craft stick long.

pencil

The water bottle is about
7 paper clips long.
It is about 2 craft sticks long.

water bottle

What should I use to measure the length of my pet goldfish?

What about a dinosaur?

Guided Learning

Complete.

3 pencil case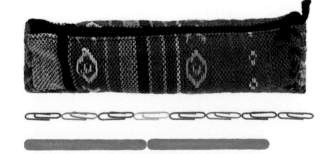

The pencil case is about ⬤ paper clips long.

It is about ⬤ craft sticks long.

 **Hands-On Activity**

Use [＿＿＿] .

STEP 1 Cut out some strips of paper.

[blank rectangle]

STEP 2 Partners use these strips to measure the length of each other's forearm.

My forearm is about [＿＿＿] strips of paper long.

STEP 3 Trace your foot on a piece of paper.

STEP 4 Use the strips of paper to measure the length of your foot.

My foot is about [＿＿＿] strips of paper long.

🖐 Hands-On Activity

Use  and  .

STEP 1 Guess how many paper clips long each strip is.

STEP 2 Then check by placing paper clips along the strips.
How many of your guesses are correct?

Which strips have the same length?
Which is the longest strip?
Which is the shortest strip?

STEP 3 Put the strips in order from longest to shortest.

Look at the picture.
Answer the questions.

1

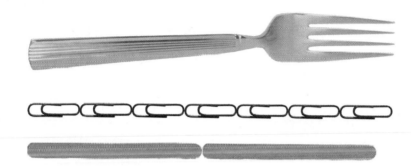

The length of the fork is about [ ] paper clips long.

It is about [ ] craft sticks long.

2 Would you use a or to

measure the window? [ ]

ON YOUR OWN

**Go to Workbook A:
Practice 4, pages 237–240**

LESSON

5 Finding Length in Units

Lesson Objectives

• Use the term "unit" to describe length.

• Count measurement units in a group of ten and ones.

Vocabulary
unit

Learn **You can measure length with units.**

1 / stands for 1 **unit**.

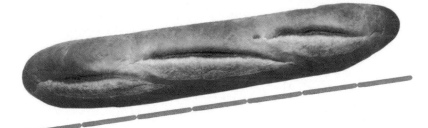

The loaf of bread is about 7 units long.

Guided Learning

Solve.

1 stands for 1 unit.

1

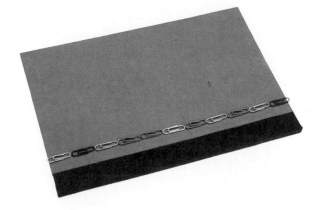

How many units long is the book? ⬜ units

You can measure length with units.

1 / stands for 1 unit.

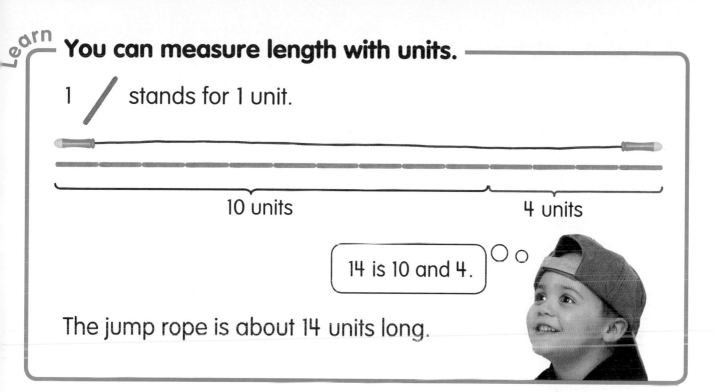

10 units   4 units

14 is 10 and 4.

The jump rope is about 14 units long.

Guided Learning

CIRCUS
SHOW

Show time: 7-9 P.M.
June 1-5

Solve.

1 / stands for 1 unit.

2 How many units long is the poster?

____ units

____ is 10 and ____.

Look at the picture.
Then answer the questions.
Each ☐ **stands for 1 unit.**

3 How long is the towel rack? ☐ units

4 How tall is the shower? ☐ units

☐ is 10 and ☐ .

5 How tall is the boy? ☐ units

☐ is ☐ and ☐ .

6 Is the brush longer than the mirror? ☐

7 Which is shorter, the brush or the towel rack? ☐

Hands-On Activity

Use ⬭ and / to measure these things in your classroom.

	⬭ stands for 1 unit	/ stands for 1 unit
computer screen		
pencil case		
doorway		
lunch box		
tissue box		

Look at the two measurements for the computer screen.

Does it take more ⬭ or / to measure its length?

Is this also true for the other things that you measured?

Why do you think this is so?

Let's Practice

Use 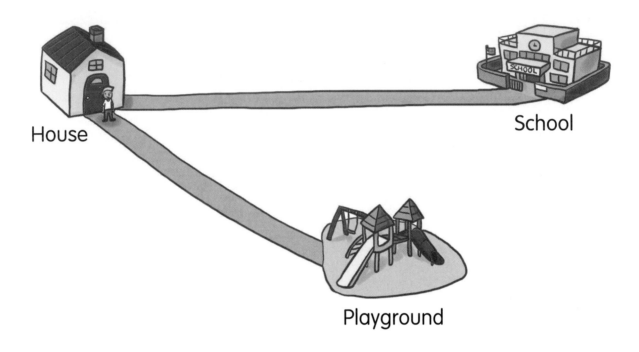 to measure.
1 paperclip stands for 1 unit.

The picture shows Chris's house, his school, and the playground.

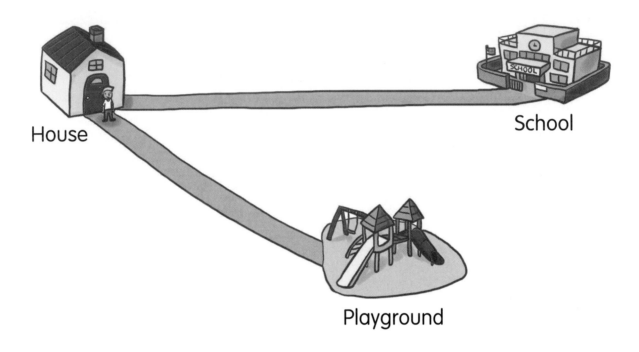

House

School

Playground

1 The sidewalk from Chris's house to school is about ⬜ units long.

2 The sidewalk from Chris's house to the playground is about ⬜ units long.

Solve.

Snails A, B, and C crawl along the lines.

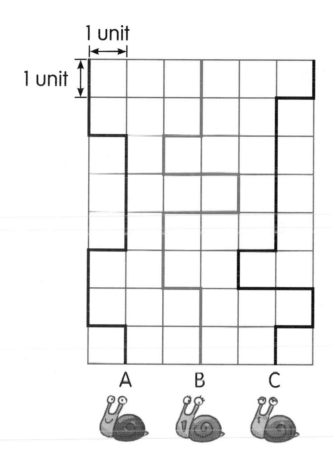

1 unit

1 unit

A   B   C

3 Which snail takes the longest path? ⬚
It crawls ⬚ units.
⬚ is ⬚ and ⬚ .

4 Which snail takes the shortest path? ⬚
It crawls ⬚ units.
⬚ is ⬚ and ⬚ .

5 Which snail crawls 13 units?
Snail ⬚ .

6 1 ☐ stands for 1 unit.

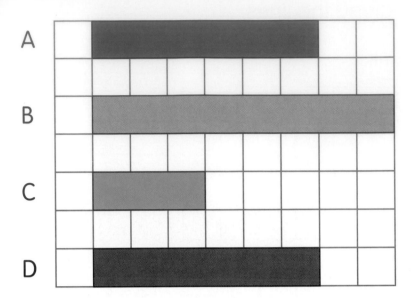

ⓐ Which is the longest strip? ⬭

ⓑ Which is the shortest strip? ⬭

ⓒ Which two strips have the same length? ⬭
They are ⬭ units long.

ON YOUR OWN

Go to Workbook A:
Practice 5, pages 241–244

CRITICAL THINKING SKILLS
Put On Your Thinking Cap!

PROBLEM SOLVING

1 Look at the loaf of bread and the book.

Can you say that the book is longer than the loaf of bread? Why?

2

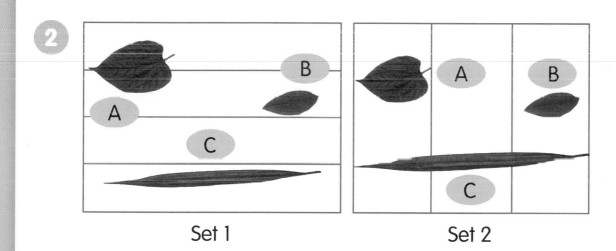

Set 1   Set 2

You want to find out how long the leaves are.
Which set of lines will you use?
Why?

ON YOUR OWN

Go to Workbook A:
Put on Your Thinking Cap!
pages 245–248

Chapter Wrap Up
You have learned...

to compare two things.

tall   taller

short   shorter

long

longer

to compare more than two things.

Ally   Ben   Carlo

Ally is taller than Ben.
Ben is taller than Carlo.
So, Ally is also taller than Carlo.

Ally is the tallest.
Carlo is the shortest.

to use a start line.

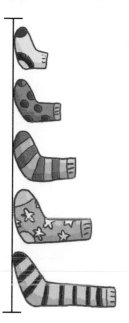

Compare the height and length of things. Measure with non-standard units to find length.

to use objects to measure.

The dog is about 10 socks long.
It is about 1 scarf long.

to use units to measure.

1  stands for 1 unit.
The cat is 2 units long.

ON YOUR OWN

Go to Workbook A:
Chapter Review/Test,
pages 249–252

Glossary

A

- **above**

  Pip is above Boo.

- **add**

  Put together two or more parts to make a whole.

  $$2 + 3 = 5$$

  part   part   whole

- **addition sentence**

  $2 + 5 = 7$ is an addition sentence.

- **addition story**

  Mary picks 4 cherries.
  June picks 5 cherries.

  $$4 + 5 = 9$$

  They pick 9 cherries in all.

- **after**

  Boo is after Wink.

- **alike**

  These shapes are circles. They are alike because they are all the same shape.

B

- **before**

Wink is before Boo.

- **behind**

Boo is behind the acorns.

- **below**

Boo is below Pip.

- **between**

Boo is between Pip and Wink.

C

- **circle**

- **color**

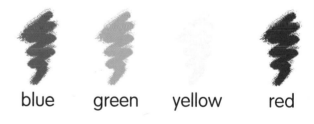

blue   green   yellow   red

- **cone**

- **corner**

  A corner is where two sides meet.

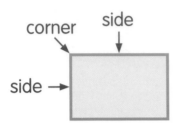

- **counting tape**

| 1 | 2 | 3 | 4 | 5 | 6 |

- **cube**

- **cyclinder**

D ————————

- **different**

  These shapes are circles. They are different because they are not the same color.

- **doubles fact**

  $$3 + 3 = 6$$

  The numbers that are added together are the same.

- **doubles plus one fact**

  $$4 + 5 = 9$$

  4 + 5 is 4 + 4 plus 1 more.

- **down**

  Pip is climbing down the tree.

E ————————

- **eight**

Count	Write	Say
	8	eight

- **eighteen**

Count	Write	Say
	18	eighteen

- **eighth**

- **eleven**

Count	Write	Say
	11	eleven

- **equal**

Having the same amount or number.

3 is the same as 2 + 1

$$3 = 3$$

↑——— equal sign

F———

- **fact family**

A group of addition and subtraction sentences that have the same parts and whole.

3 + 5 = 8	8 − 5 = 3
5 + 3 = 8	8 − 3 = 5

- **false**

5 + 4 = 10 is a false number sentence.

- **far**

Wink

Pip

Wink is far from the acorn.

- **fewer than**

There are fewer ⭐ than ❤️.

- **fifteen**

Count	Write	Say
(ten frame with 15 dots)	15	fifteen

- **fifth**

- **first**

- **five**

Count	Write	Say
(ten frame with 5 dots)	5	five

- **four**

Count	Write	Say
(ten frame with 4 dots)	4	four

- **fourteen**

Count	Write	Say
(ten frame with 14 dots)	14	fourteen

- **fourth**

- **fourth of**

  One fourth of the square is shaded.

G

- **greater than**

  4 is greater than 3.

- **greatest**

  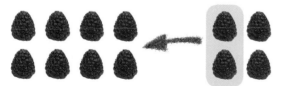

  17 is the greatest number.

- **group**

  8 raspberries   4 raspberries

  To make a group of 10 raspberries, 2 raspberries are moved.

H

- **half of**

  One half of the square is shaded.

I

- **in front of**

  Wink

  Wink is in front of the acorn.

L

- **last**

  This chipmunk is last.
  There is no one behind him.

- **least**

8 is the least number.

- **left**

Pip is on the left.

- **less than**

3 is less than 4.
3 is 1 less than 4.

- **long, longer, longest**

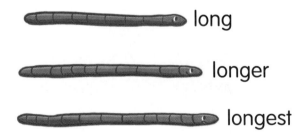

long

longer

longest

M

- **minus**

To subtract.

$$8 - 1 = 7$$

minus sign

- **more than**

There are more ⭐ than 🖤.
There is 1 more ⭐ than 🖤.

N

- **near**

Pip is near the acorn.

- **next to**

Pip   Boo   Wink

Boo is next to Pip.
Boo is also next to Wink.

- **nine**

Count	Write	Say
●●●●● ●●●●	9	nine

- **nineteen**

Count	Write	Say
●●●●● ●●●●● ●●●●● ●●●●	19	nineteen

- **ninth**

- **number bond**

part

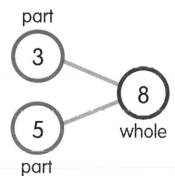

3

5

8

whole

part

A number bond shows parts and the whole.
Parts make up a whole.
You can use a number bond to help you add or subtract.

- **number words**

  zero   eight
  sixteen   twenty

- **numbers**

  0   1   16   20

O

- **one**

Count	Write	Say
	1	one

- **order**

  You can order numbers from least to greatest or greatest to least.

  4   7   11   20

  least

  20   11   7   4

  greatest

P

- **part**

  See **number bond**.

- **pattern**

  number patterns
  - 2, 4, 6, 8, 10
  - 20, 19, 18, 17, 16

  a shape pattern

- **place-value chart**

  A place-value chart shows how many tens and ones are in a number.

  In the number 19, there is 1 ten and 9 ones.

Tens	Ones
1	9

- **plus**

  To add.

$$10 + 1 = 11$$

  plus sign

- **pyramid**

Q

- **quarter of**

One quarter of the square is shaded.

R

- **rectangle**

- **rectangular prism**

- **repeating pattern**

A pattern that happens again and again...

square, circle, square, circle …

- **right**

Wink is on the right.

- **roll**

S

- **same**

4 stars

4 hearts

same number

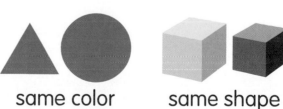

same color   same shape

- **second**

- **seven**

Count	Write	Say
	7	seven

- **seventeen**

Count	Write	Say
	17	seventeen

- **seventh**

- **shape**

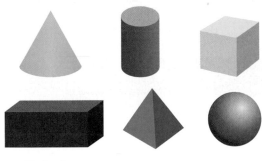

plane shapes

solid shapes

- **short, shorter, shortest**

short   shorter   shortest

side

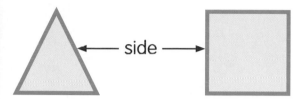

A triangle has 3 sides.
A square has 4 sides.

six

Count	Write	Say
	6	six

sixteen

Count	Write	Say
	16	sixteen

sixth

Free Acorns!

size

small   big

slide

sphere

square

stack

start line

You can use a start line to compare the length of things.

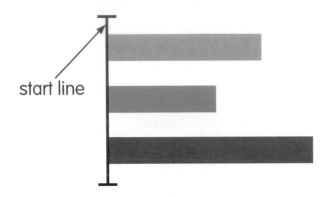

start line

subtract

Take away one part from the whole to find the other part.

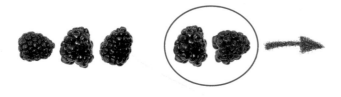

5 − 2 = 3
whole part part

subtraction sentence

7 − 3 = 4 is a subtraction sentence.

subtraction story

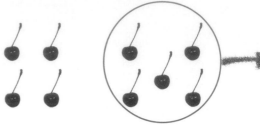

Mary has 9 cherries.
June eats 5 cherries
9 − 5 = 4
Mary has 4 cherries left.

T

take away

See **subtract**.

tall, taller, tallest

tall   taller   tallest

ten

Count	Write	Say
●●●●● ●●●●●	10	ten

- **tenth**

- **third**

- **thirteen**

Count	Write	Say
●●●●● ●●●●● ●●●	13	thirteen

- **three**

Count	Write	Say
●●●	3	three

- **triangle**

- **true**

  5 + 4 = 9 is a true number sentence.

- **twelve**

Count	Write	Say
●●●●● ●●●●● ●●	12	twelve

- **twenty**

Count	Write	Say
●●●●● ●●●●● ●●●●● ●●●●●	20	twenty

- **two**

Count	Write	Say
	2	two

U

- **under**

Pip

Pip is under the leaf.

- **unit**

Units are used to measure things.

 can be used to measure.

1 stands for 1 unit.

The pencil is 6 units long.

- **up**

Pip is climbing up the tree.

W

- **whole**

  See **number bond**.

Z

- **zero**

Count	Write	Say
	0	zero

Index

Pages listed in regular type refer to Student Book A.
Pages listed in blue type refer to Student Book B.
Pages in *italic type* refer to Workbook (WB) A.
Pages listed in *blue italic type* refer to Workbook (WB) B.
Pages in **boldface** type show where a term is introduced.

Pages listed in regular type refer to Student Book A.
Pages listed in blue type refer to Student Book B.
Pages in *italic type* refer to Workbook (WB) A.
Pages listed in *blue italic type* refer to Workbook (WB) B.
Pages in **boldface** type show where a term is introduced.

using symbols >, <, and =, 196, **204**, 205, 211, 215, WB 153

    weight, *See* Weight

Compose a ten to add 2-digit numbers, *See* Regrouping

Composing numbers, *See* Number bonds; Place value; *and* Regrouping

Computers, 124, 136, 238

Cone, *See* Geometric shapes

Congruent shapes, *See* Geometric shapes

Connecting cubes, *See* Manipulatives

Corner, *See* Geometric shapes

Counters, *See* Manipulatives

Counting

    0 to 10, 4–7, 9, 11–12, 27, 169–170, 30, 46, 50, 53; *WB 1–6, 7–11, 35, 259; WB 45, 141–142, 185*

    11 to 20, 171–174, 175, 181–182, 196; 53, 55; *WB 167–172, 193–194, 253; WB 45, 141–142, 185*

    21 to 40, 57– 62, 179; *WB 45–47, 49–50, 141–147, 185–187*

    to 120, 180–192, 305; *WB 141–142, 144–147, 187*

    back, *See* Ones, Patterns, and Subtraction

    estimate, **186**, 191, 309; *WB 144, 159, 160, 186*

    making a ten, **174**, 176, 53, 58, 61, 179, 175, 183–186, 191; *WB 45–48, 59, 145–147, 185–188, 263*

    on, See Addition, strategies; Money; Patterns; *and* Subtraction, strategies

    and place value, 183, 53, 55, 58–61, 63–65, 193–195; *WB 173–174, 176, WB 45, 49–50, 60–62, 93–94, 141–142, 144–145, 185, 187, 263*

    related to addition and subtraction, 42, 43, 44, 45, 47–48, 49, 171, 174, 84, 87, 89–93, 96–98, 101–102, 104–105, 110, 132–133, 221–222, 227, 234–235, 241, 250–251; *WB 41–44, 46, 68–69, 90, ; WB 61–64, 87, 161, 189–190*

Counters, *See* Manipulatives

Counting tape, *See* Addition *and* Subtraction

Critical Thinking and Problem Solving, *See* Problem solving, Put on Your Thinking Cap!

Cube, *See* Geometric shapes

Cumulative Review, *See* Assessment

Cylinder, *See* Geometric shapes

Data, **30**

    collect/count, 30, 36–37, 42, 46, 48, 50; *WB 29–30, 35, 37–38, 44, 91*

    compare, 31–35, 37–41, 47–49; *WB 25–29, 31–34, 35–37, 39, 43–44, 90*

    interpret, 32–35, 38–41, 49, 50; *WB 25–26, 31–34, 40, 43–44, 90, 249, 269*

    organize, **36**, 42; *WB 38, 42, 44*

    represent data, 31–41, 43–49, **50**, 157–158, 160–161; *WB 29–30, 35, 37–38, 44, 91*

    show

        as picture graph, **31**, 44; *WB 25–34, 90–91*

        in a bar graph, 42, 45, 51; *WB 37, 40, 42–44, 91*

        in a tally chart, 42–43; *WB 35–37, 40, 43–44, 91*

        with pictures, 28–30; *WB 35–37*

    understand, 36, 38, 50; *WB 25–34, 39–44, 90, 249, 269*

Date, *See* Calendar

Days, *See* Calendar

Dimes, *See* Coins

Division readiness, 254–264, *WB 199–213, 215–216*

    concept of, 252, 257

    and groups, 254–256, 259

        each group, 254–258, 260–261, 264; *WB 202–203, 214*

        equal groups, 254–258, 260–261, 264; *WB 198, 206*

        greatest number of groups, 267

    same number, 254–255, 257, 259, 261, 265, 314

    share equally, **259**, 261–262, 268; *WB 194–197*

Doubles fact, *See* Addition, strategies; *and* Subtraction, strategies

Doubles plus one, *See* Addition, strategies

Drawings, *throughout. See for example*, 63, 132, 163–165, 179–180, 238, 253, 28–51, 53, 83–84, 113, 115, 119–120, 129, 136–137, 200, 226, 228, 265, 267–268; *WB 18, 51, 64, 92, 156, 175, 188, WB 40, 42, 62, 78, 103, 106, 139*

    bar graphs, 37–41, 44, 49–50; *WB 37, 40, 42–44, 91*

    diagrams, 63, 163–165, 253, 131, 176, 267; *WB 156, 189, 245–247, WB 39, 106*

    number lines, *See* Number Line

End of Year Review, *See* Assessment
Equal, Equality, **260**
    equal amount, *See* Money
    equal groups, *See* Division readiness
    equal sign (=), **42**, *throughout. See for example,* 44,
        49, 79, 53, 60, 65
    equal value, *See* Money
    sharing equally, *See* Division
Equations (add WB)
    addition, *See* Addition, addition sentences
    subtraction, *See* Subtraction, subtraction sentences
    true and false, *See* Algebraic thinking
    number sentences to represent real-world problems
        addition sentences, 51–52, 54–57, 59–61, 64–65,
          90, 201, 215–218, 223, *123–124,128–131,*
          258, 298–299; WB 55–56, 59–61, 89,
          91–92, 258, 260; WB 79–82, 98, 182
        subtraction sentences, 69–70, 72, 79–85, 89,
          96–97, 215–218, 223, *124–127, 130–131,*
          298–299; WB 87–88, WB 79–82, 98, 171,
          242–244, 251, 254
Estimate, *See* Counting
Exploration
    Let's Explore!, 10, 35–36, 94, 125, 162, 180, 220, 230,
        121–122, 142, 148, 212, 257, 265, 300

Fact families, *See* Addition and Subtraction
False equations, *See* Algebraic thinking

Games, *See* Activities
Geometric shapes, 98–143, 267; *WB 97–142*
    attributes, 102–104, 109, 116, 118–119
    defining, *See* sorting and classifying; number of
        corners; *and* number of sides
    nondefining, *See* sorting and classifying; color; *and*
        size

combining, 122, 123, 124–125, 127–128, 129, 143,
    WB 111–116, 117–118, 134–135
composite, 122, 123, 124–125, 127–128, 129;
    WB 111–116, 117–118
concrete models, 107, 111, 119, 124–125, 127–129, 132, 139
congruent, 109–111; *WB 103–104, 142, 166*
corners, **103**, 109–111, 142; *WB 101–103, 139, 161, 260*
decomposing a whole, 112, 113, 114, 115, 143;
    WB 103–106, 115, 134–135, 142, 161
equal parts
fourth of, fourths (quarter), **113**, 114–115, 143, 266;
    WB 105–106, 140
half of, halves, **112**, 114–115, 125, 143, 262; *WB 105–106*
moving solid shapes, 118–121, *WB 109–110*
    roll, rolling, **118**, 119, 121, 142, 266; *WB 109–110, 131, 140,*
        162, 261
    slide, sliding, **118**, 119, 121, 142, 268; *WB 109, 131, 140–141,*
        162, 261
    stack, stacking, **118**, 119, 121, 142, 268; *WB 109, 131, 162*
orientation, 102–103, 106–107, 117, 121–122, 125–127, 129–131,
    133–134; *WB 99, 102, 108–110*
patterns, 100–101, 135–141, 143, 265, *WB 117–126*
    completing, 136–137, 139–141; *WB 124–128, 129–130,*
        137–138, 142, 156, 163, 166
    creating, 136, 139, *WB 127–128, 132, 156*
    describing, 135, 138
    extending, *See* completing
    repeating, **135**, 136–141, 143, 266; *WB 124–130, 137–138,*
        142, 156, 163, 166
partitioning, *See* equal parts
plane (two-dimensional shapes), 267
    circle, 100–101, **102**, 108–109, 114, 123, 125–126, 130–134,
        135–137; *WB 97–102, 111–114, 116*
    closed, 100–109, 112–115, 122–126, 135–137; *WB 93–96,*
        105–110, 133, 156, 261
    compose, 110, 114,115, 122, 123, 124, 125; *WB 112–113,*
        115–116, 134–135, 137–139,
    rectangle, 100–101, **102**, 108–109, 114, 122–126, 130–134,
        135–137, 266; *WB 97–102, 111–114, 139, 161–162,*
        261
    square, 100–101, **102**, 108–109, 112–113, 122–126, 131–133,
        135–137, 268; *WB 97–100, 111–114, 116, 139,*
        161–162, 261; WB 214, 264
    trapezoid, 108
    triangle, 100–101, **102**, 108–109, 112, 114–115, 122–126,
        131–133, 135–137, 270; *WB 97–101, 111–116, 139, 161,*
        261; WB 214, 268

Pages listed in regular type refer to Student Book A.
Pages listed in blue type refer to Student Book B.
Pages in *italic type* refer to Workbook (WB) A.
Pages listed in *blue italic type* refer to Workbook (WB) B.
Pages in **boldface** type show where a term is introduced.

ordering, 235, 244, 265; *WB 235*

short, **227–228**, 230, 254, 267; *WB 244, 249*

shorter, **227–228**, 229–231, 239, 249, 254, 267; 5;
*WB 225–229, 231–232, 242–244, 252, 256–257,
267*

shortest, **233**, 234–236, 238–239, 241, 244, 251–252,
254, 267; 3, 5; *WB 230–231, 235, 243–246,
249–250, 252, 256, 266*

start line, **237**, 238–239, 255, 269; *WB 235–236, 257, 267*

tall, **227**, 229, 231–232, 235–236, 254, 269; *WB 250, 252,
264*

taller, **227**, 229, 231–232, 235–236, 254, 269; 3;
WB 225–229, 231–232, 244, 246, 252, 256

tallest, **233**, 234–236, 239, 254, 269; 3, 5; *WB 230–231,
244, 246–247, 252, 256, 264*

using a grid unit, 248, 251–253, 271; *WB 243–245*

Let's Explore!, *See* Exploration

Let's Practice, *throughout. See for example,* 12, 53, 78, 108,
140, 205, 236, 250

Light, Lighter, Lightest, *See* Weight

(M)

Manipulatives
attribute blocks, 107, 126
base-ten blocks, 174, 178–180, 183–185, 196–197, 58–61,
63–64, 69, 179, 185, 193, 214; *WB 170; WB 47,
49–50, 59, 147*

balance, 32–33, 35, 38; 8, 11, 15, 19, 20; *WB 34, WB 1–14,
16–19, 21–24*

classroom objects
apple, 15, 19
beans,
green, 94–95, 111–112
red, 94–95, 111–112
book, *WB 5*
calculator, 11
candle, 20
clothes pins, 15
craft sticks, 240–242, 246–248, 250, 64, 194
crayons, 8, 20
eraser, 8, 19
index cards, 162
leaf, 8

markers, 15
metal spoon, 11,
modeling clay, 11
orange, *WB 5*
paper, 244, 248; *WB 5*
paper clips, 240, 242, 244, 246–247, 250–253, 8,
19–20; *WB 5*
pencil, 8, 19
pencil case, 15, 20
plastic bottle, 11
sharpener, 8
scarf, 19,
scissors, 11, 19; *WB 5*
wallet, 8
computers, *See* Technology
connecting cubes, *throughout. See for example* 4–6,
16–17, 20, 22–25, 30, 33, 125, 265;
counters, *throughout. See for example* 10, 17, 21, 24, 26,
44, 51, 246–247, 256–257, 260; *WB 35, 39, 43, 89*
geometric solids, 117, 127–129, 132, 143
hundred chart, 198, 212; *WB 157–158*
math balance, *See* balance
number cards, 76–77, 141, 147, 213
number cube, 94–95, 111–112, 236–237
play money
coin tokens, 293
spinners, 147, 200
Math balance, *See* Manipulatives
Math Journal, *See* Communication
Measure *and* Measurement, *See* Length; Time; *and* Weight,
Mental math, 134–151, *WB 99–104, 107–108, 135–136, 264*
Mid-Year Review, *See* Assessment
Minus, *See* Subtraction
Minute hand, *See* Time
Missing addend, *See* Addition
Missing minuend, *See* Subtraction
Missing subtrahend, *See* Subtraction
Models, *See also* Addition; Geometric Shapes; Numbers;
Pictorial models; Problem solving strategies; *and*
Subtraction
abstract, *throughout. See for example,* 42, 50–57, 59–61,
64–65, 69, 79–82, 84–87, 96, 163, 177–180,
203–208, 53, 81–82, 84, 121–122, 131, 135–151, 188,
192, 229, 275–277, 284, 286–287, 289–290, 294,

Pages listed in regular type refer to Student Book A.
Pages listed in blue type refer to Student Book B.
Pages in *italic type* refer to Workbook (WB) A.
Pages listed in *blue italic type* refer to Workbook (WB) B.
Pages in **boldface** type show where a term is introduced.

Pages listed in regular type refer to Student Book A.
Pages listed in blue type refer to Student Book B.
Pages in *italic type* refer to Workbook (WB) A.
Pages listed in *blue italic type* refer to Workbook (WB) B.
Pages in **boldface** type show where a term is introduced.

situations
    take away (taking from, taking apart), 69–71, 76–80,
        85, 96; *WB 65–68, 89, 92–93*
    comparing, 169–170, 183–184, 197, 124–127, 130–131,
        298–299
    stories, **79**, 80–83, 96–97, 269, 124–127, 130–131,
        298–299; *WB 77–84, 91–92, 217–218, 258, 268,*
        WB 79–82, 104, 108, 242–244, 251, 254
strategies
    counting back, 74–75, 96, 101–102, 104–105, 133,
        234–235, 251, 307; *WB 65–70, 90, WB 69, 171,*
        190
    counting on, 69, 72–75, 96; *WB 68, 90*
    group into a ten and ones, 209–212, 219, 222–223,
        145–146; *WB 209–216, 223, 254, WB 69–71, 73,*
        103–104, 267
    doubles facts, **206**, 212, 214, 218, 223, 259;
        WB 223–224
    number bonds, 67–68, 76–80, 84–85, 87, 96–97, 214,
        219, 223, 264, 102–103, 106–107, 114, 116–117,
        135, 137, 143–147, 151; *WB 71–76, 93, 209–216,*
        263, WB 103–104
    number line, **196**, 197, 199–200, 206–207
    related to addition 87–93, 97, 212; 82–83, 143, 149,
        219; *WB 84, 88, 94, 96, 260, WB 103–104, 107*
    subtrahend, missing, 77–80, 82, 84–85, 88, 90, 93, 200,
        217–218; *WB 84, 89–90, 92, 219, 260*
    unknown addend, 88, 90, 93, 97
    with zero, 81; *WB 66, 73, 76, 81, 90*
Symbols
    >, 196, **204**, 205, 211, 215; *WB 153*
    <, 196, **204**, 205, 211, 215; *WB 153*
    =, 42, *throughout. See for example,* 51, 91, 176, 203, 223,
        260, 53, 55, 65, 74, 89, 195, 298
    in picture graphs, *See* Picture graphs

Taking away (taking from, taking apart), *See* Subtraction,
    strategies
Tally chart, **42**, 43–44, 46, 48, 51, 315; *WB 35–37, 40, 43–44,*
    270
    tally mark, **42**, 43–44, 46, 48, 315; *WB 35–37, 40, 43–44,*
    91, 270

Technology
    computers, 124, 136, 238
Tens and ones, *See* Ones
Thinking Skills
    analyzing parts and whole, 37, 63, 94–95, 220–221;
        76–77, 131, 176, 213, 267, 302–303; *WB 31–32,*
        59–60, 87–88, 190, 219–220, WB 181
    analyzing patterns and relationships, 195; *WB 18, 137–138*
    classifying, 26, 133, 141; 49; *WB 17, 133, 137–138, WB 214*
    comparing, 26, 253; 23, 49, 76–77, 213, 267, 302–303;
        WB 17, 31–32, 137–138, 153, 189–191, 219–220,
        245–247; WB 39–42, 105–106, 248, 250–251
    deduction, 37, 63, 163–165, 253; 249; *WB 31–32, 59–60,*
        88, 154–155, 189–191, 245–246
    identifying patterns and relationships, 141; 150, 249, 267;
        WB 18, 137–138, 156, 221, WB 58, 182
    identifying relationships, 163–165; *WB 83*
    induction, 247
    interpreting data, *WB 40, 125, 249*
    sequencing, 164, 23, 76–77; *WB 153, 155, 247; WB 57, 83,*
        130, 252
    spatial visualization, *WB 133–135, WB 247*
Three-dimensional shapes (cubes, right rectangular prisms,
        right circular cones, and right circular cylinders),
        See Geometric shapes, solid
Time, **152**, 164–177; *WB 113–124, 130–133, 137–138*
    afternoon, 171; *WB 128*
    clock, 152, **164**, 166–168, 171–174, 177; *WB 113–124, 130,*
        132–133, 137–138
        clock hands, **164**, 167; *WB 131*
        digital, **164**, 166, 169, 170, 173, 175
        hour hand, **164**, 170, 176; *WB 131*
        minute hand, **164**, 170, 176; *WB 131*
        use clocks to show times; *WB 118, 122, 138*
    half hour, **170**, 171–175; *WB 121–124, 126–128, 130–133,*
        137–138
    half past, **170**, 171–177; *WB 121–124, 127–128, 131–132,*
        137–138
    hour, 164–166, 169, 173; *WB 113–124, 130–133, 137–138*
    minute, 166, 173; WB 131
    morning, 168, 170–171, 175; *WB 128*
    night, 171, 174; *WB 128*
    o'clock, **164**, 164–177; *WB 113–118, 121, 123–124, 127–128,*
        131–132, 137–138, 261, 266
    show, 164, 166–167, 169, 174–175; *WB 118, 120*

Pages listed in regular type refer to Student Book A.
Pages listed in blue type refer to Student Book B.
Pages in *italic type* refer to Workbook (WB) A.
Pages listed in *blue italic type* refer to Workbook (WB) B.
Pages in **boldface** type show where a term is introduced.

Photo Credits

Acknowledgements

The publisher wishes to thank the following organizations for sponsoring the various objects used in this book:

Accent Living
Flower frames p. 4
Plate with fish motifs p. 61
Spoons p. 88

Growing Fun Pte Ltd
Math balance pp. 32, 35, 38

Hasbro Singapore Pte Ltd
For supplying Play-Doh™
to make the following:
    Clay stars p. 211
    Clay cats pp. 60, 96
    Clay shells p. 216

Lyves & Company Pte Ltd
Fish mobile p. 237

Noble International Pte Ltd
Unit cubes – appear throughout the book

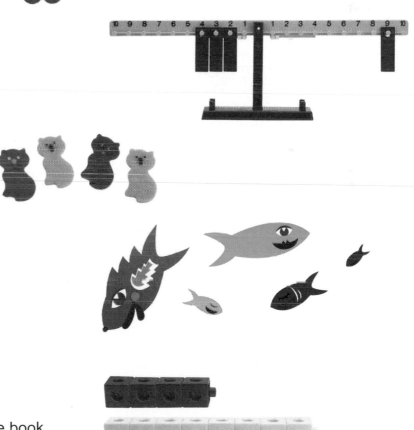

The publisher also wishes to thank the individuals who have contributed in one way or another, namely:
Model Isabella Gilbert
And all those who have kindly loaned the publisher items for the photographs featured.

COMMON CORE STATE STANDARDS FOR MATHEMATICAL CONTENT

STANDARD	DESCRIPTOR	PAGE CITATIONS
1.OA OPERATIONS AND ALGEBRAIC THINKING		
Represent and solve problems involving addition and subtraction		
1.OA.1	Use addition and subtraction within 20 to solve word problems involving situations of adding to, taking from, putting together, taking apart, and comparing, with unknowns in all positions, e.g., by using objects, drawings, and equations with a symbol for the unknown number to represent the problem.	SE 1A: 42–45, 59–62, 69–78A, 84–86, 87–93, 198–200, 215–220 SE 1B: 123–131, 143–149
1.OA.2	Solve word problems that call for addition of three whole numbers whose sum is less than or equal to 20, e.g., by using objects, drawings, and equations with a symbol for the unknown number to represent the problem.	SE 1A: 215–220 SE 1B: 123–131, 267
Understand and apply properties of operations and the relationship between addition and subtraction		
1.OA.3	Apply properties of operations as strategies to add and subtract.	SE 1A: 30–36, 42–54, 55–58, 198–200, 220–221 SE 1B: 119–122, 134–137, 138–142, 143–149, 150
1.OA.4	Understand subtraction as an unknown-addend problem.	SE 1A: 69–78A, 79–83, 84–86, 87–93, 94–95, 201–204, 209–214, 215–220 SE 1B: 101–110, 111–118, 123–131, 134–137, 234–241, 242–248
Add and subtract within 20		
1.OA.5	Relate counting to addition and subtraction (e.g., by counting on 2 to add 2).	SE 1A: 42–54, 55–58, 69–78A, 189–194 SE 1B: 57–62, 84–93, 182–192, 196–212

COMMON CORE STATE STANDARDS FOR MATHEMATICAL CONTENT

STANDARD	DESCRIPTOR	PAGE CITATIONS
1.OA.6	Add and subtract within 20, demonstrating fluency for addition and subtraction within 10. Use strategies such as counting on; making ten (e.g., $8 + 6 = 8 + 2 + 4 = 10 + 4 = 14$); decomposing a number leading to a ten (e.g., $13 - 4 = 13 - 3 - 1 = 10 - 1 = 9$); using the relationship between addition and subtraction (e.g., knowing that $8 + 4 = 12$, one knows $12 - 8 = 4$); and creating equivalent but easier or known sums (e.g., adding $6 + 7$ by creating the known equivalent $6 + 6 + 1 = 12 + 1 = 13$).	SE 1A: 37, 55–58, 59–62, 69–78A, 79–83, 84–86, 87–95, 201–208 SE 1B: 80–83, 119–122, 123–131, 138–142, 143–149, 252–253

Work with addition and subtraction equations

STANDARD	DESCRIPTOR	PAGE CITATIONS
1.OA.7	Understand the meaning of the equal sign, and determine if equations involving addition and subtraction are true or false.	SE 1A: 42–54, 55–58, 59–62, 63, 69–78A, 79–83, 84–86, 87–93, 94–95, 201–208, 209–214, 215–220 SE 1B: 84–93, 101–110, 111–118, 119–122, 123–131, 138–142, 143–149, 221–227, 228–233, 234–241, 242–248, 254–258, 296–301
1.OA.8	Determine the unknown whole number in an addition or subtraction equation relating to three whole numbers.	SE 1A: 42–54, 59–62, 63, 84–86, 87–95, 201–208, 209–214 SE 1B: 13–17, 18–22, 30–35, 36–41, 57–62, 63–65, 66–75, 84–93, 94–100, 111–118, 119–122, 123–131, 134–137, 138–142, 143–149, 221–227, 228–233, 234–241, 242–248

1.NBT NUMBER AND OPERATIONS IN BASE TEN

Extend the counting sequence

STANDARD	DESCRIPTOR	PAGE CITATIONS
1.NBT.1	Count to 120, starting at any number less than 120. In this range, read and write numerals and represent a number of objects with a written numeral.	SE 1A: 4–12, 20–26, 171–176, 177–180, 189–194 SE 1B: 52–56, 57–62, 63–65, 66–77, 178–181, 182–192, 193–195, 196–212

COMMON CORE STATE STANDARDS FOR MATHEMATICAL CONTENT

STANDARD	DESCRIPTOR	PAGE CITATIONS
Understand place value		
1.NBT.2	Understand that the two digits of a two-digit number represent amounts of tens and ones. Understand the following as special cases:	
1.NBT.2.a	10 can be thought of as a bundle of ten ones — called a "ten."	SE 1A: 171–176, 177–180, 181–188 SE 1B: 57–62, 63–65, 66–75, 84–93, 94–100, 111–118, 182–192, 193–195, 196–212, 221–227, 228–233, 234–241, 242–248
1.NBT.2.b	The numbers from 11 to 19 are composed of a ten and one, two, three, four, five, six, seven, eight, or nine ones.	SE 1A: 171–176, 177–180, 181–188, 189–194
1.NBT.2.c	The numbers 10, 20, 30, 40, 50, 60, 70, 80, 90 refer to one, two, three, four, five, six, seven, eight, or nine tens (and 0 ones).	SE 1B: 57–62, 63–65, 84–93, 182–192, 193–195, 196–212, 221–227, 234–241
1.NBT.3	Compare two two-digit numbers based on meanings of the tens and ones digits, recording the results of comparisons with the symbols >, =, and <.	SE 1A: 181–186, 189–194, 224–226 SE 1B: 66–75, 178–181, 196–212
Use place value understanding and properties of operations to add and subtract		
1.NBT.4	Add within 100, including adding a two-digit number and a one-digit number, and adding a two-digit number and a multiple of 10, using concrete models or drawings and strategies based on place value, properties of operations, and/or the relationship between addition and subtraction; relate the strategy to a written method and explain the reasoning used. Understand that in adding two-digit numbers, one adds tens and tens, ones and ones; and sometimes it is necessary to compose a ten	SE 1B: 84–93, 94–100, 111–118, 123–131, 138–142, 143–149, 216–220, 221–227, 228–233, 234–241, 242–248

COMMON CORE STATE STANDARDS FOR MATHEMATICAL CONTENT

STANDARD	DESCRIPTOR	PAGE CITATIONS
1.NBT.5	Given a two digit number, mentally find 10 more or 10 less than the number, without having to count; explain the reasoning used.	SE 1B: 138–142, 143–149
1.NBT.6	Subtract multiples of 10 in the range 10-90 from multiples of 10 in the range 10-90 (positive or zero differences), using concrete models or drawings and strategies based on place value, properties of operations, and/or the relationship between addition and subtraction; relate the strategy to a written method and explain the reasoning used.	SE 1B: 101–110, 111–118, 234–241

1.MD MEASUREMENT AND DATA

Measure lengths indirectly and by iterating length units

1.MD.1	Order three objects by length; compare the lengths of two objects indirectly by using a third object.	SE 1A: 232–236, 246–252, 253 SE 1B: 1–5
1.MD.2	Express the length of an object as a whole number of length units, by laying multiple copies of a shorter object (the length unit) end to end; understand that the length measurement of an object is the number of same-size length units that span it with no gaps or overlaps. Limit to contexts where the object being measured is spanned by a whole number of length units with no gaps or overlaps.	SE 1A: 240–245, 246–252 SE 1B: 1–5

Tell and write time

1. MD.3	Tell and write time in hours and half-hours using analog and digital clocks.	SE 1B: 164–169, 170–175, 176

Represent and interpret data

1.MD.4	Organize, represent, and interpret data with up to three categories; ask and answer questions about the total number of data points, how many in each category, and how many more or less are in one category than in another.	SE 1B: 30–35, 36–41, 49

1.G GEOMETRY

Reason with shapes and their attributes

1.G.1	Distinguish between defining attributes (e.g., triangles are closed and three-sided) versus non-defining attributes (e.g., color, orientation, overall size); build and draw shapes to possess defining attributes.	SE 1A: 102–115, 141

COMMON CORE STATE STANDARDS FOR MATHEMATICAL CONTENT

STANDARD	DESCRIPTOR	PAGE CITATIONS
1.G.2	Compose two-dimensional shapes (rectangles, squares, trapezoids, triangles, half-circles, and quarter-circles) or three-dimensional shapes (cubes, right rectangular prisms, right circular cones, and right circular cylinders) to create a composite shape, and compose new shapes from the composite shape.	SE 1A: 102–115, 122–129
1.G.3	Partition circles and rectangles into two and four equal shares, describe the shares using the words *halves*, *fourths*, and *quarters*, and use the phrases *half of*, *fourth of*, and *quarter of*. Describe the whole as two of, or four of the shares. Understand for these examples that decomposing into more equal shares creates smaller shares.	SE 1A: 102–115, 122–129

 # COMMON CORE STATE STANDARDS FOR MATHEMATICAL PRACTICE

STANDARDS	PAGE CITATIONS
1. MAKE SENSE OF PROBLEMS AND PERSEVERE IN SOLVING THEM.	

How *Math in Focus*® Aligns: ***Math in Focus*®** is built around the Singapore Ministry of Education's mathematics framework pentagon, which places mathematical problem solving at the core of the curriculum. Encircling the pentagon are the skills and knowledge needed to develop successful problem solvers, with concepts, skills, and processes building a foundation for attitudes and metacognition. ***Math in Focus*®** is based on the premise that in order for students to persevere and solve both routine and non-routine problems, they need to be given tools that they can use consistently and successfully. They need to understand both the *how* and the *why* of math so that they can self-monitor and become empowered problem solvers. This in turn spurs positive attitudes that allow students to solidify their learning and enjoy mathematics. ***Math in Focus*®** teaches content through a problem solving perspective. Strong emphasis is placed on the concrete-to-pictorial-to-abstract progress to solve and master problems. This leads to strong conceptual understanding. Problem solving is embedded throughout the program.	*For example:* SE 1A: 4–12, 20–26, 30–36, 37, 59–62, 63, 87–93, 94–95, 102–115, 130–134, 138–140, 141, 151–163, 163–165, 189–194, 195, 215–220, 220–221, 246–252 SE 1B: 18–22, 23, 36–41, 49, 66–75, 76–77, 94–100, 101–110, 123–131, 143–149, 150, 170–175, 176, 213, 242–248, 249, 254–258, 263–266, 267, 296–301, 302–303

STANDARDS	PAGE CITATIONS

2. REASON ABSTRACTLY AND QUANTITATIVELY.

How *Math in Focus*® Aligns:

***Math in Focus*®** concrete-pictorial-abstract progression helps students effectively contextualize and decontextualize situations by developing a deep mastery of concepts. Each topic is approached with the expectation that students will understand both *how* it works, and also *why*. Students start by experiencing the concept through hands-on manipulative use. Then, they must translate what they learned in the concrete stage into a visual representation of the concept. Finally, once they have gained a strong understanding, they are able to represent the concept abstractly. Once students reach the abstract stage, they have had enough exposure to the concept and they are able to manipulate it and apply it in multiple contexts. They are also able to extend and make inferences; this prepares them for success in more advanced levels of mathematics. They are able to both use the symbols and also understand why they work, which allows students to relate them to other situations and apply them effectively.

For example:

SE 1A: 20–26, 30–36, 42–54, 55–58, 59–62, 63, 87–93, 94–95, 138–140, 141, 151–163, 163–165, 189–194, 195, 215–220, 220–221, 232–236, 237–239, 246–252

SE 1B: 6–12, 18–22, 36–41, 66–75, 76–77, 101–110, 119 122, 123–131, 143–149, 150, 164–169, 170–175, 176, 182–192, 213, 242–248, 249, 254–258, 263–266, 296–301, 302–303

3. CONSTRUCT VIABLE ARGUMENTS AND CRITIQUE THE REASONING OF OTHERS.

How *Math in Focus*® Aligns:

As seen on the Singapore Mathematics Framework pentagon, metacognition is a foundational part of the Singapore curriculum. Students are taught to self-monitor, so they can determine whether or not their solutions make sense. Journal questions and other opportunities to explain their thinking are found throughout the program. Students are systematically taught to use visual diagrams to represent mathematical relationships in such a way as to not only accurately solve problems, but also to justify their answers. Chapters conclude with a Put on Your Thinking Cap! problem. This is a comprehensive opportunity for students to apply concepts and present viable arguments. Games, explorations, and hands-on activities are also strategically placed in chapters when students are learning concepts. During these collaborative experiences, students interact with one another to construct viable arguments and critique the reasoning of others in a constructive manner. In addition, thought bubbles provide tutorial guidance throughout the entire Student Book. These scaffolded dialogues help students articulate concepts, check for understanding, analyze, justify conclusions, and self-regulate if necessary.

For example:

SE 1A: 4–12, 30–36, 87–93, 102–115, 122–129, 151–163, 215–220, 227–231

SE 1B: 119–122, 138–142, 143 149, 196–212, 254–258, 263–266, 296–301

STANDARDS	PAGE CITATIONS

4. MODEL WITH MATHEMATICS.

How *Math in Focus*® Aligns:

Math in Focus® follows a concrete-pictorial-abstract progression, introducing concepts first with physical manipulatives or objects, then moving to pictorial representation, and finally on to abstract symbols. A number of models are found throughout the program that support the pictorial stage of learning. *Math in Focus*® places a strong emphasis on number and number relationships, using place-value manipulatives and place-value charts to model concepts consistently throughout the program. In all grades, operations are modeled with place-value materials so students understand how the standard algorithms work. Even the mental math instruction uses understanding of place value to model how mental arithmetic can be understood and done. These place-value models build throughout the program to cover increasingly complex concepts. Singapore Math® is also known for its use of model drawing, often called "bar modeling" in the U.S. Model drawing is a systematic method of representing word problems and number relationships that is explicitly taught beginning in Grade 2 and extends all the way to secondary school. Students are taught to use rectangular "bars" to represent the relationship between known and unknown numerical quantities and to solve problems related to these quantities. This gives students the tools to develop mastery and tackle problems as they become increasingly more complex.

For example:

SE 1A: 37, 42–54, 59–62, 63, 69–78A, 79–83, 84–86, 87–93, 102–115, 116–121, 122–129, 130–134, 138–140, 163–165, 201–208, 215–220

SE 1B: 23, 49, 84–93, 94–100, 101–110, 111–118, 119–122, 123–131, 196–212, 213, 221–227, 228–233, 234–241, 242–248, 267, 302–303

5. USE APPROPRIATE TOOLS STRATEGICALLY.

How *Math in Focus*® Aligns:

Math in Focus® helps students explore the different mathematical tools that are available to them. New concepts are introduced using concrete objects, which help students break down concepts to develop mastery. They learn how to use these manipulatives to attain a better understanding of the problem and solve it appropriately. *Math in Focus*® includes representative pictures and icons as well as thought bubbles that model the thought processes students should use with the tools. Several examples are listed below. Additional tools referenced and used in the program include clocks, money, dot paper, place-value charts, geometric tools, and figures.

For example:

SE 1A: 4–12, 13–19, 20–26, 30–36, 42–54, 87–93, 102–115, 122–129, 135–137, 163–165, 171–176, 177–180, 181–188, 237–239, 240–245, 246–252

SE 1B: 6–12, 13–17, 18–22, 23, 49, 57–62, 63–65, 66–75, 94–100, 111–118, 119–122, 123–131, 138–142, 143–149, 176, 182–192, 193–195, 196–212, 242–248, 254–258, 286–295, 302–303

COMMON CORE STATE STANDARDS FOR MATHEMATICAL PRACTICE

STANDARDS	PAGE CITATIONS

6. ATTEND TO PRECISION.

How *Math in Focus*® Aligns:

As seen in the Singapore Mathematics Framework, metacognition, or the ability to monitor one's own thinking, is key in Singapore Math®. This is modeled for students throughout **Math in Focus**® through the use of thought bubbles, journal writing, and prompts to explain reasoning. When students are taught to monitor their own thinking, they are better able to attend to precision, as they consistently ask themselves, "does this make sense?" This questioning requires students to be able to understand and explain their reasoning to others, as well as catch mistakes early on and identify when incorrect labels or units have been used. Additionally, precise language is an important aspect of **Math in Focus**®. Students attend to the precision of language with terms like factor, quotient, difference, and capacity.

For example:

SE 1A: 4–12, 42–54, 69–78A, 87–93, 102–115, 122–129, 151–163, 171–176, 209–214, 215–220, 227–231

SE 1B: 94–100, 111–118, 119–122, 129, 138–142, 143–149, 242–248, 249, 254–258, 263–266, 286–295, 296–301

7. LOOK FOR AND MAKE USE OF STRUCTURE.

How *Math in Focus*® Aligns:

The inherent pedagogy of Singapore Math® allows students to look for, and make use of, structure. Place value is one of the underlying principles in **Math in Focus**®. Concepts in the program start simple and grow in complexity throughout the chapter, year, and grade. This helps students master the structure of a given skill, see its utility, and advance to higher levels. Many of the models in the program, particularly number bonds and bar models, allow students to easily see patterns within concepts and make inferences. As students progress through grade levels, this level of structure becomes more advanced.

For example:

SE 1A: 26, 87–93, 141, 189–194, 220–221

SE 1B: 18–22, 66–75, 76–77, 150, 249, 267

8. LOOK FOR AND EXPRESS REGULARITY IN REPEATED REASONING.

How *Math in Focus*® Aligns:

A strong foundation in place value, combined with modeling tools such as bar modeling and number bonds, gives students the foundation they need to look for and express regularity in repeated reasoning. Operations are taught with place value materials so students understand how the standard algorithms work in all grades. Even the mental math instruction uses understanding of place value to model how mental arithmetic can be understood and done. This allows students to learn shortcuts for solving problems and understand why they work. Additionally, because students are given consistent tools for solving problems, they have the opportunity to see the similarities in how different problems are solved and understand efficient means for solving them. Throughout the program, students see regularity with the reasoning and patterns between the four key operations. Students continually evaluate the reasonableness of solutions throughout the program; the consistent models for solving, checking, and self-regulation help them validate their answers.

For example:

SE 1A: 20–26, 30–36, 42–54, 59–62, 69–78A, 79–83, 84–86, 87–93, 171–176, 189–194, 195, 209–214, 215–220

SE 1B: 76–77, 84–93, 94–100, 101–110, 111–118, 119–122, 123–131, 138–142, 143–149, 213, 221–227, 228–233, 234–241, 242–248, 254–258

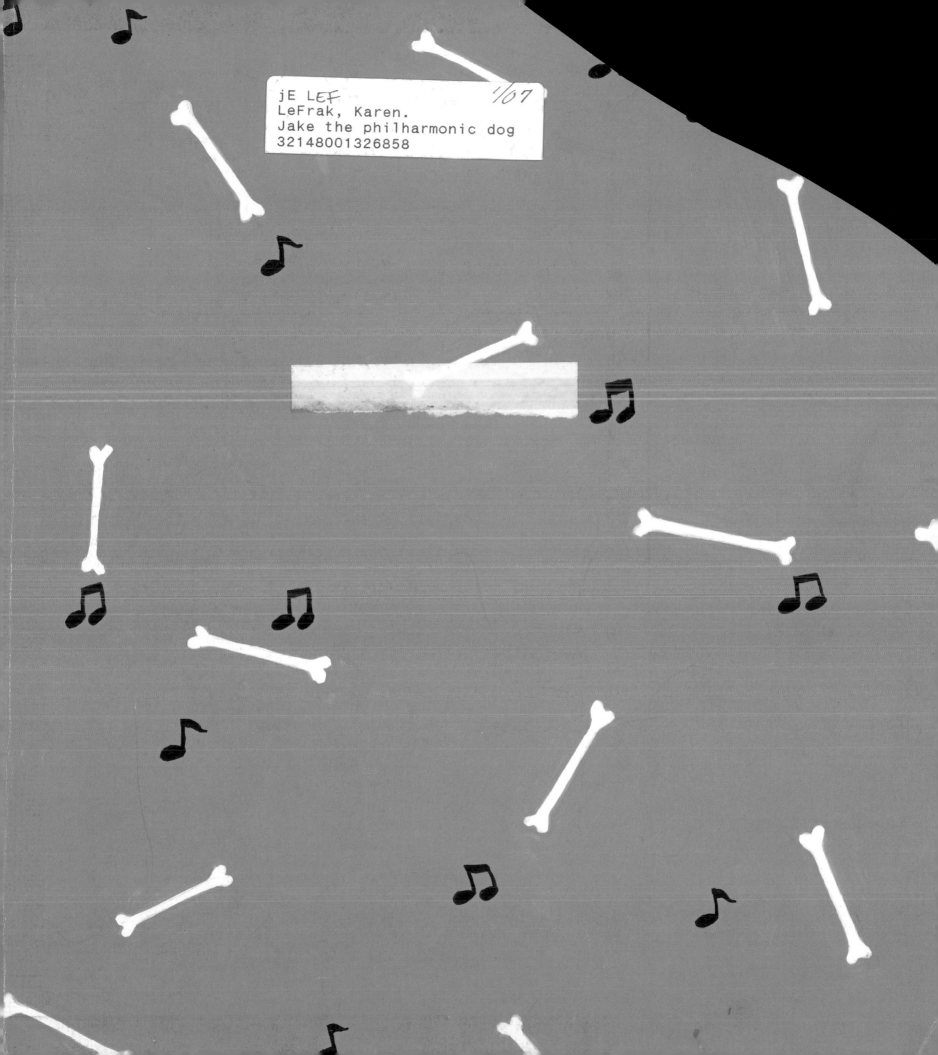